Worship: The Christian's Highest Calling

WORSHIP
THE CHRISTIAN'S HIGHEST CALLING

MARK SWEETNAM

Copyright © Scripture Teaching Library and Mark S. Sweetnam, 2013.

ISBN: 978-1-909789-10-4

All rights reserved. No part of this publication may be reproduced, stored in or introduced into a retrieval system, or transmitted, in any form or by any means (electronic, mechanical, photocopying, recording or otherwise), without the prior written permission of the copyright owner.

Printed by Kingsbridge Press Ltd, Cookstown, Northern Ireland.
Cover image: Noah's Thank Offering (c. 1803) by Joseph Anton Koch, Wikimedia Commons.

Preface

The nucleus of this book was a series of articles that appeared in *Believers Magazine* from March to August 2012. I am grateful to the editor, John Grant, for extending to me the hospitality of the magazine, and for his permission to reprint the material in this form. I am grateful to all those who have commented helpfully on those articles and on this volume. I am deeply indebted to the saints in the assembly in Rathmines, Dublin, for the warmth of their fellowship and their encouragement as I engaged with the various aspects of this subject. As always, my thanks are due to Sara and Josiah for all their love and support. Much of this book was written while Sara was undergoing extensive hospitalisation, and I would like to take this opportunity to thank the many believers in many places who so faithfully remembered us in prayer. May this book be used to the glory of 'Him that is able to do exceeding abundantly above all that we ask or think, according to the power that worketh in us, Unto Him be glory in the church by Christ Jesus throughout all ages, world without end. Amen.'

Mark Sweetnam
Dublin, 2013

Contents

1	Worship Defined	11
2	Worship Desired	17
3	Worship Dispensationally	21
4	Worship and its Dimensions	43
5	Worship Directed	49
6	Worship Delivered	55
7	Worship Displayed	63
8	Worship Depicted	77
9	Worship Developed	83
10	Worship Demonstrated (I)	91
11	Worship Demonstrated (II)	99
12	Worship Demonstrated (III)	115

Give unto the LORD the glory due unto His name: bring an offering, and come before Him: worship the LORD in the beauty of holiness.

1 Chronicles 16:29

Give unto the LORD the glory due unto His name; worship the LORD in the beauty of holiness.

Psalm 29:2

O worship the LORD in the beauty of holiness: fear before Him, all the earth.

Psalm 96:9

Except where otherwise indicated, all quotations from Scripture are taken from the Authorised (King James) Version.

Chapter 1

Worship Defined

In the world of contemporary evangelicalism a great deal is said about worship. Outside countless ecclesiastical buildings countless notice boards advertise worship services. Many of the gatherings that meet in these buildings find use for the services of a worship leader. The shelves of Christian bookshops groan beneath the weight of CDs and DVDs whose liners invite us to become part of a 'world of worship', to share in a 'worship experience'. On the surface, there seems to be no shortage of worship.

However, a closer examination of this 'worship industry' leaves little scope for complacency. Indeed, it quickly becomes apparent that much of what is packaged and sold as worship is very different from the pattern of worship provided in Scripture. In the narcissistic emotionalism of its content, the unscriptural banality of its lyrics – with their seemingly endless repetition – in its aping of the music of the world and its glorification of individual musicians or 'worship leaders' this 'worship' falls very far short of anything mandated by the Word of God. That such a distorted and deformed substitute should, in the eyes of God's people, pass for real worship is indicative of a serious failure to grasp the true nature of worship as presented in the Word of God.

When studying any scriptural concept, it is often helpful to begin by looking at the passage of Scripture where the concept is introduced for the first time. Our endeavour to understand scriptural worship takes us to Genesis 18:

> And the LORD appeared unto him in the plains of Mamre: and he sat in the tent door in the heat of the day; And he lift up his eyes and looked, and, lo, three men stood by him: and when he saw them, he ran to meet them from the tent door, and bowed himself toward the ground, And said, My LORD, if now I have found favour in Thy sight, pass not away, I pray thee, from Thy servant (vv. 1–3).

The word 'worship' does not appear in the English translation of this passage. However, the word translated 'bowed himself' is the word most commonly translated as 'worship' in the Old Testament. This passage, then, could be said to present us with a prototype of scriptural worship and it has important lessons for us about the motivation, the attitude, the object and the consequences of true worship.

THE MOTIVATION INVOLVED

First of all, we should notice the motivation behind Abraham's act of worship. We could imagine a number of circumstances in which the patriarch might have been moved to bow down before these strangers. Had they presented the threat of physical danger, he might have bowed in supplication, to beg them for favour. Had they bestowed some gift upon him, he might have bowed as an expression of gratitude. This account presents neither of these motivations. Abraham had nothing to fear from these men and he had, at this stage, received nothing from them. His act of humility was motivated purely and simply by his recognition that he was in the presence of Someone greater than he.

That should be the motivation for our worship too. There are three chief ways in which we approach God. We come to Him with prayer and supplication to ask for His help and blessing. We return with thanksgiving and praise when we receive that blessing. But worship transcends any purely personal considerations. It has to do with Who and What God is, and not with ourselves. It is the fervent, heartfelt acknowledgement of His worth. In the words of J.N. Darby 'It is the honour and adoration which are rendered to God, by reason of what He is in Himself, and what He is for those who render it. Worship is the employment of heaven; and a blessed and precious privilege for us upon earth, if the enjoyment of it be vouchsafed to us.'[*] Rightly has it been described as the Christian's highest occupation.

THE ATTITUDE EXPRESSED

This understanding of the motivation of worship will inevitably inform the attitude in which that worship is offered. In both Hebrew and Greek, worship is a postural term that speaks of the complete abnegation of self. When Abraham bowed himself before the Lord he was making a dramatic statement about the relative importance of himself and the One he worshipped. He was of no significance, and so he abased himself. True worship must always adopt this attitude spiritually. It is the least selfish, least egotistical activity known to humankind. Any talk of 'worship experience' misses this crucial point. Such terminology turns the spotlight back on the self, its feelings, emotions and responses.

[*] J.N. Darby, *Collected Works*, 7:88

True worship, by distinction, is not motivated by what we receive, or what we feel, but by what we can give as we acknowledge the absolute, extraordinary and unparalleled worth of the One to Whom our worship is directed.

THE OBJECT ADDRESSED

If this is what worship is, it should be very apparent that it cannot be lightly offered, nor are many worthy of it. Indeed, while our fellow men may command our respect, attract our affections or our love, we do not find in them the value that makes them fit objects of our worship. Only God, in the greatness of His person, is worthy of worship. This is indicated in this first mention of worship. In Genesis 18 it was Jehovah Who appeared to Abraham. The passage records a Christophany, a pre-incarnation appearance of the Son of God. So, Abraham bowed, not before an ordinary – or extraordinary – man, but before the Son of God. It is worth noting that it is He Who receives the first worship recorded in Old and New Testaments (Mt. 2:2). Mankind as a whole has crucially failed in ascribing the worship due to God alone to lesser entities. How careful we should be to ensure that we follow the example of Abraham in directing our worship only to the Father and the Son.

THE CONSEQUENCES ENJOYED

Abraham's worship was not an isolated or self-contained act. Rather, it had consequences well beyond itself. Firstly, it led to service. As Abraham straightened himself from the ground, he immediately sought to minister to his visitors, describing himself as 'thy servant' (significantly in the singular). Worship should always come before service. This is true in the sense of priority. Worship must precede service – it is an incongruous thing if brethren's voices are often heard in the preaching of the gospel or the teaching of the Word while they consistently sit silent on a Lord's Day morning. But worship also comes before service in the sense of motivation. Abraham's recognition and acknowledgement of the worth of his visitor engendered in him a burning desire to serve. Indeed, one of the Hebrew words translated by worship can be, and sometimes is translated as 'serve'. Nor is this link difficult to substantiate in the New Testament. The familiar words of Romans 12:1 exhort us:

> I beseech you therefore, brethren, by the mercies of God, that ye present your bodies a living sacrifice, holy, acceptable unto God, which is your reasonable service.

The offering of a living sacrifice is an act of worship: at the same time it is our logical service to God. It should not be a strange thing that our worship should lead us to serve more fervently. Indeed, it would be very strange if we could contemplate the greatness of our Saviour and not be moved to love Him more and serve Him better.

It was another consequence of Abraham's worship that he gained a fresh understanding of God. It was in the atmosphere and aftermath of his worship that he received a renewal of God's promise. This was followed by a revelation of God's purpose in relation to the cities of the plain, and by a remarkable experience in prayer. For Abraham, worship deepened communion with God. True worship always will, for it causes us to learn more about God and to enjoy more fully the reality of our relationship with Him.

In the example of Abraham, we see worship as God defines and desires it. In the light of this patriarchal prototype, how does our worship compare? Individually and collectively we have both the opportunity and the responsibility to worship God. He seeks worshippers (Jn 4:23) and He seeks worship. It is our highest activity, part of the purpose for which we have been saved. It is our shame and our loss, if we accept any substitute for worship in its reality. It is incumbent upon us to ensure that what we offer is in accordance with His will and in keeping with His person.

CHAPTER 2

WORSHIP DESIRED

THE RECORD OF the encounter of the Lord Jesus with the woman of Samaria in John chapter four is a particularly moving portion of God's Word. In it we see the Creator of the world sitting weary on the well. We see His love and grace displayed to a woman who was an open and notorious sinner. We learn something of the perfectly balanced humanity and Deity of Christ in her invitation to her neighbours to 'come see a man ... is not this the Christ?' (Jn 4:29). Strikingly, it is in this context and to this woman that the Lord Jesus reveals fundamental truth about the nature of worship and its importance. Refusing to be distracted by a debate about historical and theological disputes, He cuts right to the heart of true worship in the dispensation of grace. True worship is no longer limited by location or ethnicity, but it must be offered 'in spirit and in truth' (v. 24). And, speaking of true worshippers, He adds 'the Father seeketh such to worship Him'.

ANGELS

God has always desired the worship of His creatures. He seeks –and receives – it from angels. Isaiah and

John, among others, record for us the reality of angelic worship. Hebrews 1:6 records His desire concerning His Son: 'let all the angels of God worship him'. It could hardly be otherwise. Dwelling in the light of His presence and privileged to witness the outworkings of His purposes, they could scarcely fail to respond with worship to the greatness of God.

HUMANITY

But, as the Saviour revealed to the Samaritan woman, God also seeks the worship of humanity. Indeed, this is part of His design for mankind. Romans 2 makes it clear that God has implanted in humanity the capacity to worship, to recognise and respond to that which is greater than we are. The revelation of God's greatness and goodness furnished to us in the splendours of His Creation was designed as a prompt and stimulus for that innate and God-given capacity. But, as with all that was good in man, the Fall has fundamentally compromised our capacity for worship. It has been abased, no longer directed at the Creator God, but at creation. Man no longer worships that which is higher than himself. At best, worship has become merely horizontal – the acclamation and adoration of some man or woman. All too often it has been directed down, to the lower parts of creation, to the beasts, and to inanimate and corrupting possessions. Its natural bent is no longer upwards. But for all this, God's desire has not altered, and still He seeks true worshippers to worship Him.

THE JEWS

From the Jews, too, God sought worship. The tabernacle and the temple were both the prompt and the place of worship. Designed in every detail to represent the person of Christ they demonstrated, in a tangible way, the intensity of Divine holiness and the splendour of Divine glory. And, while the offerings that were made there addressed the guilt of sin and expressed the thankfulness of the blessed, they made provision too, and in greater part, for the worship of God. These offerings, unlike the sacrifices offered to pagan gods, were not offered to curry Divine favour or to avert Divine disfavour. Rather, the offerer approached with his offering as an indication – concrete and costly – of his appreciation of the ineffable greatness of the God Who sought and savoured the worship of His chosen people.

Once again, man failed to give to God the worship that He desires and deserves. Even in the earliest days of the nation's history the Israelites engaged in defective worship. It was mistaken in its object at Sinai as they worshipped the golden calf. It was rebellious in its disobedience as Nadab and Abihu offered 'strange fire' (Lev. 10). And, in the book of Malachi, it was defective in its value, and the prophet had to upbraid the nation for their robbery of God and for what this counterfeit of worship revealed about their false understanding of the character of Jehovah. In each of these instances, it is solemn to note, the consequences of defective worship were serious. God did not take lightly man's failure correctly to worship Him, and He views such failure no less seriously today.

THE CHURCH

The Father still seeks worshippers. But the worship that He desires is not haphazard. It finds neither its form nor its content in the human imagination. The requirement to worship in Jerusalem is no longer in force. In the dispensation of grace we can worship wherever we wish. But we cannot worship however we wish. God desires worship in spirit and in truth.

The importance and the seriousness of worship is a truth that we too often lose sight of. We must ever guard against offering to God the strange fire of innovation that, in the world of contemporary evangelicalism, has transformed worship into elaborately produced, flesh directed, egocentric emotionalism. It should be our constant exercise to ensure that we worship in truth – in accordance with the precept and pattern of the New Testament. It is equally vital to ensure that we worship in spirit. In Malachi's day, the form of worship was impeccably correct. No complaint could have been made regarding the place of sacrifice or the mode of its offering. For all that, it was offensive to God because it was only second best. How often we, too, fail here, offering to God the dregs of our life, the corners of our mind, the tatters of our time?

If we fail in this way, we fail for precisely the same reason as the Israelites did. They lost sight of the greatness of God. When we, like them, allow the world and its materialism to strangle and stunt our knowledge of God and our communion with Him, it becomes easy – even routine – to offer to him the lame, the blemished and the mediocre.

The day is coming when the knowledge of God will be universal (Hab. 2:14). Consequently, all creation will be united in the worship of God (Zech. 14:16, Isa. 66:23). From every valley and hill, from every cranny of creation, true worship will resound, fuller and freer than ever before. Until then the Father seeks worshippers. Let us, by His grace, resolve that in our life, at least, He will not seek in vain.

CHAPTER 3

WORSHIP DISPENSATIONALLY

THROUGHOUT HISTORY, God has sought worship from humanity. The vast majority of mankind failed to respond to His revelation by offering to Him the worship that He desired (Rom. 1:25). But in every age, there have been found those who have bowed their knees and hearts, and have worshipped God.

It is striking, even on a very cursory reading of Scripture, that the form of worship offered to God has differed from age to age. The sacrifices that were offered on the temporary altars constructed by godly men from Abel, down through the patriarchs, differed dramatically from the complex and comprehensive system of sacrifice and offering that was implemented under the Law, and that focused first on the Tabernacle and then on the Temple. That system was itself brought to a dramatic end when the Roman siege of AD 70 culminated in the storming of the city and the destruction of the Temple. In this age, the ceremony of the Temple has been replaced by the simplicity of New Testament worship. And, while the difference between the worship that preceded the giving of the Law, and that which followed it is striking, the contrast between Levitical and Christian worship is far more radical. No longer is worship linked to a particular geographical centre. No longer are animal sacrifices laid on the altar to be consumed by its flames. The psalteries, harps, and cymbals have fallen silent. The change in worship has been so fundamental, so dramatic that the thoughtful reader of Scripture must, almost inevitably, ask why such a change has taken place.

We find the answer to this question in John chapter four. There, as the Lord Jesus spoke to the Samaritan woman, He outlined the radical changes that were about to take place in the nature of worship:

> Jesus saith unto her, Woman, believe me, the hour cometh, when ye shall neither in this mountain, nor yet at Jerusalem, worship the Father. Ye worship ye know not what: we know what we worship: for salvation is of the Jews. But the hour cometh, and now is, when the true worshippers shall worship the Father in spirit and in truth: for the Father seeketh such to worship Him. God is a Spirit: and they that worship Him must worship Him in spirit and in truth (Jn 4:21–24).

With these words, the Saviour drew a contrast between two types of worship. In the context, we might well have expected that He would speak at length of the difference between the worship of God in the Temple, and the syncretistic facsimile of worship offered by the Samaritans. But those differences receive only the briefest of mentions: 'Ye worship ye know not what: we know what we worship.' The real focus of the Saviour's words is the difference between a form of worship that is passing, and one that will shortly be inaugurated. With the phrase 'the hour cometh', the Lord Jesus drew the woman's attention to an impending change in the way that God would be worshipped.* A new dispensation would require a new type of worship.

In these verses, the Lord Jesus mentions four contrasts between the old worship and the new. The first of these is a geographical contrast. The worship of the passing dispensation was geographically confined. The Samaritans had erroneously linked worship with Mount Gerizim, and the Jews with Jerusalem. But that would all change. In the new dispensation what would matter was Who and how people worshipped, not where.

It is important to notice that the contrast between the present and future is continued throughout these verses. The Lord Jesus is not primarily articulating general principles about worship in these verses, though that is, to some extent, the case. Rather, He is speaking about the nature of worship that God will seek when the hour is come, how true worshippers *will* worship, anticipating a change that will come to pass.

This becomes clear when we look in a little more detail at the expression 'true worshippers', which draws the second contrast between the worship of the passing dispensation and that which was about to dawn. It is important to grasp that the contrast here is not between truth and falsehood. The worship offered to God under the Levitical system was not false worship – it could not be, for it had been Divinely prescribed. But the word for truth in this passage does not mean truth as opposed to falsehood. Rather, it signifies genuine, as opposed to the 'imperfect, shadowy, or insubstantial'.† The worship of the Jews at Jerusalem and, even more so, of the Samaritans at Mount Gerizim, was partial and

---

* This characteristically Johannine phrase occurs on seven occasions in his gospel: 4:21, 23; 5:25, 28; and 16:2, 25, 32.

† J.H. Bernard, *A Critical and Exegetical Commentary on the Gospel according to St John*, (Edinburgh: T. & T. Clark, 1999), I, 11

provisional. The Temple, in all its glory and with all its elaborate ceremony, was only a limited, shadowy pointer to far greater realities. The ritual of sacrifice and offering carried out over so many centuries had no innate or inherent virtue. Now, it would all be done away, and worshippers of God would move from the shadow to the substance, from the type to the antitype, from the partial to the perfect.

There is a sense in which this seems counter-intuitive. After all, the worship associated with the Tabernacle and Temple had a material, physical reality. In these structures, the holiness of God was given tangible expression, real blood was shed, real animals offered, and consumed by real flames. And yet, from God's perspective, these physical entities were only 'the example and shadow of heavenly things'. The ordinances and rituals of the Levitical system were only the 'shadow of things to come' (Col. 2:17). These true worshipers would abandon the material for the immaterial, but in doing so they would, paradoxically, be leaving the shadow for the substance.

It is worth pausing to summarise what we have seen so far. Speaking to the Samaritan woman, the Lord Jesus predicts an imminent alteration in the way in which God was to be worshiped. Worship would no longer be linked with a single geographical location – the debates between the Jews and the Samaritans on that score would shortly become irrelevant. And this worship would be offered by genuine worshippers, who would participate in a spiritual reality that had previously only been foreshadowed by the Law.

Then, the Lord Jesus provides two crucial details about the sort of worship that would be offered in the new dispensation and by these genuine worshippers. They would worship 'in spirit and in truth'. These two expressions provide two further contrasts between worship as it had been known, and as it would be known. Both of these expressions have generated a certain amount of debate, and both are deserving of careful attention.

Of the two terms, the latter is, perhaps, the easier to understand. In spite of what some commentators have suggested, the phrase does not refer to the sincerity of our worship. Our worship should be authentic, not a mere ritual or performance. This is absolutely and fundamentally vital, and sadly, many of us would have to confess with shame that this is not always the case in our own experience. But it is not the sincerity of the individual worshipper that is in view here. Again, it is important to remember that a contrast is being drawn. It is certainly not the case that worshippers in the dispensation of law were not sincere in their worship – examples could be multiplied that would abundantly prove otherwise. Worship 'in truth' means far more than that.

'Truth' is one of the most important concepts in John's gospel – as a noun or an adjective it occurs on forty-eight occasions (compared to sixty-one occurrences in all of Paul's writings, and just ten in the synoptic gospels). It is linked with each of the persons of the Godhead. So, in John 17:17, the Lord Jesus prayed to His Father 'Sanctify them through Thy truth: Thy Word is truth'. The Lord Jesus was (and is) 'full of grace and truth' (1:14), and 'grace and truth came by' Him (1:17). He described Himself to the Jews as 'a man that hath told you the truth, which I have heard of God' (8:40). And, in John 14:6, He declared 'I am the way, the truth, and the life.' In John 15:26 and John 16:13, He speaks of the Spirit of truth, Who would guide the disciples into 'all truth'. The possession of the truth is the hallmark of true believers in the Lord Jesus Christ. He promised 'ye shall know the truth, and the truth shall make you free' (8:32). Those who believe on Him are indwelt by 'the Spirit of truth' (14:17), are guided by Him 'into all truth' (16:13), are 'sanctified through [the] truth' (17:17, 19), and are 'of the truth' (18:37). Truth, in John's gospel, originates with God, is revealed in Christ, and is apprehended by the power of the Holy Spirit.

The worshippers of the coming dispensation would worship in truth. Worship is linked with revelation, and only now, 'in these last days' when God has 'spoken unto us by His Son' (Heb. 1:2) can mankind worship God in truth, in all its fullness. It may well be that the Lord Jesus is contrasting this worship with that offered by the Samaritans who did not know what – or Who – they worshipped. There is certainly a marked contrast between these genuine worshippers and those of whom Paul spoke in Romans 1:25, 'who changed the truth of God into a lie, and worshipped and served the creature more than the Creator, who is blessed for ever.'

Let us remember that for us, the hour of which the Saviour spoke has already come. In this dispensation of grace, the Father seeks those who will worship Him, in the fulness of truth. Our worship must not be based on our own fallacious notions about God, but it must arise from what He has revealed of Himself to us. And, as we learn in this very gospel, we find that truth in Christ, Who is 'the Truth', recorded in His Word, which 'is truth', and under the guidance of 'the Spirit of truth'. The Father seeks theologically intelligent worship, worship that is formed, and fuelled, and fed by the Scriptures, that arises from an understanding and appreciation of God that owes nothing to the imaginations or philosophies of man, and everything to the Word of God. This is the sort of worship that God accepts. Indeed, it is the worship that He seeks. Does He find it in our lives?

The Father seeks worship 'in truth', but also 'in spirit'. The precise interpretation and implications of this expression have caused some debate. Some commentators suggest that it is the Holy Spirit Who is referred to here, that God seeks worship 'in Spirit' – that is, in the energy and power of the Holy Spirit. This is undoubtedly true. In Philippians 3:3, for example, Paul describes the believers of this dispensation as 'the circumcision, who worship by the Spirit of God, and boast in Christ Jesus, and do not trust in flesh'(*Darby*). It is not, however, altogether clear that this interpretation fully exhausts the meaning of what the Lord is saying here. Others see this as a reference to the spirit of the individual, and suggest that the Saviour is describing the fervency of the worship that God desires, not a dreary mechanical exercise, but something vital. Again, this is undeniably true, but again this does not seem to be the most likely interpretation of the passage.

Our understanding of the true meaning of this phrase will be greatly assisted if we pay attention to the following verse: 'God is spirit, and the people who worship Him must worship in spirit and truth' (Jn 4:24, NET). With these words, the Lord Jesus explains why it is necessary that God *must* be worshipped 'in spirit and in truth.' God, He tells us, 'is spirit'. That is, He is a spiritual being. His existence is not material or physical. And this truth about the nature of God has implications for the way in which He must be worshipped. Physical worship may befit a material idol, but a God Who is spirit must be worshipped in a spiritual way.

This truth was stressed twice over at the commencement of the dispensation of grace. Speaking to a Jewish audience, Stephen reminded his hearers of the transcendence of God:

> Howbeit the most high dwelleth not in temples made with hands; as saith the prophet, Heaven is My throne, and earth is My footstool: what house will ye build Me? saith the Lord: or what is the place of My rest? Hath not My hand made all these things? (Acts 7:47–50)

Stephen's reference to the words of 'the prophet' would have reminded those who listened of two portions of Old Testament Scripture. Their minds would have gone back to the words of Solomon as he embarked on the construction of the Temple:

> And the house which I build is great: for great is our God above all gods. But who is able to build Him an house, seeing the heaven and heaven of heavens cannot contain Him? Who am I then, that I should build Him an house, save only to burn sacrifice before him? (2 Chron. 2:5–6).

Even as preparations were being taken in hand for the building that would be the crowning glory of the Levitical system of worship, the king acknowledged that concrete material worship could never be sufficient, that it was possible only because of God's condescension in accommodating Himself to human frailty.

More solemnly, the minds of the Jews would have gone to the words of Isaiah:

> Thus saith the LORD, The heaven is My throne, and the earth is My footstool: where is the house that ye build unto Me? And where is the place of

> My rest? For all those things hath Mine hand made, and all those things have been, saith the LORD: but to this man will I look, even to him that is poor and of a contrite spirit, and trembleth at My word. He that killeth an ox is as if he slew a man; he that sacrificeth a lamb, as if he cut off a dog's neck; he that offereth an oblation, as if he offered swine's blood; he that burneth incense, as if he blessed an idol. Yea, they have chosen their own ways, and their soul delighteth in their abominations (Isa. 66:1–3).

The prophet's words were a stark warning of the dangers of an externally correct formal worship that was utterly without spiritual reality. Those who listened to Stephen's address would surely have understood – and no doubt resented – the point that Stephen was making. Their fathers had been judged for their idolatrous worship of 'Moloch and the star of [their] god Remphan' (Acts 7:43), and while the worship that these Jews were involved in was formally exact, they too had departed from the true, spiritual worship of God. The worship 'in spirit' of which the Lord Jesus spoke to the Samaritan woman was utterly antithetical to the reality of what happened in the Temple.

Stephen's message to the Jews was echoed to the Gentiles by the Apostle Paul. Speaking on Mars Hill, to those who worshipped 'THE UNKNOWN GOD', he alluded to the same Scripture:

> God that made the world and all things therein, seeing that He is Lord of heaven and earth, dwelleth not in temples made with hands; Neither is worshipped with men's hands, as though He needed any thing, seeing He giveth to all life, and breath, and all things. ... Forasmuch then as we are

> the offspring of God, we ought not to think that the Godhead is like unto gold, or silver, or stone, graven by art and man's device. And the times of this ignorance God winked at; but now commandeth all men every where to repent: (Acts 17:24–25, 29–30).

These Gentiles offered the wrong sort of worship because they had a wrong understanding of the nature of God. Supposing that 'the Godhead' is like that which can be 'graven by art, and man's device', they followed their mistake to its logical conclusion, and worshipped 'with men's hands'. Just as worship 'in spirit' stood in total opposition to the empty formalism of Jewish worship, so, too, was it distinct from the mistaken worship of the Gentiles. These Greeks, with their learning, philosophy, and vaunted civilisation worshiped neither in spirit nor in truth.

The truth that God desires worship 'in spirit' is vital in its importance and far-reaching in its implications. In this dispensation, all of the physical and sensual worship of earlier dispensations has been left behind. The sights, the sounds, and the smells that made the worship of Levitical system so appealing to the flesh, and that have – for precisely this reason – been adopted by so much of Christendom have no place in this dispensation. Genuine worshippers now worship without geographical distinction, and they do so 'in spirit and in truth', and the Father still seeks 'such people to be His worshippers' (Jn 4:23, NET).

It is important to understand that there is nothing arbitrary about the change in worship that the Lord Jesus described. Rather, the contrasts that He outlined to the Samaritan woman are an essential part of the nature of the dispensation that was about to dawn. Worship, work, and warfare in this new dispensation would all be spiritual in their character. And this change was only made possible by the descent and indwelling of the Holy Spirit at Pentecost. That unprecedented event is anticipated in this chapter in the Saviour's words concerning the 'well of water springing up into everlasting life' (v.14) that He would give to those who asked it of Him, and it is clearly and comprehensively predicted later in the gospel (14:17, 16:13). The indwelling of the Holy Spirit had a profound impact on every aspect of the believer's life. It is His power that makes it both possible and necessary for us to worship in spirit, without the prompts and props of the Levitical system.

Similarly, it is only in the dispensation of grace that worship in truth becomes really possible. In earlier dispensations, God's people had only a partial revelation. The rich typical meaning of the sacrifices and offerings, of the furniture and fittings of the Tabernacle and Temple that are so precious to us with the benefit of New Testament hindsight were hidden to them. They worshipped, but the true spiritual significance of their worship eluded them. Only now, in the day of grace, with the completed revelation of God, embodied in His Son, and communicated by the Holy Spirit can we worship God in truth.

This dispensational change affects every area of the worship of God. The spiritual nature of worship in the present dispensation has profound implications for the sanctuary, the priesthood, and the sacrifices of believers in the Church Age.

'A Spiritual House'

Under the Law, the worship of God had, as its focus, a specific structure in which God deigned to dwell. The Tabernacle and the Temple were architecturally rather distinctive, and their construction and contents were remarkable. Their true significance, however, lay not in the details of their design, but in the fact that God deigned to dwell there, in the midst of His people. The descent of the 'glory of the LORD' upon the Tabernacle (Exod. 40:34) was one of the most remarkable moments in the history of the nation of Israel, for it signalled God's presence amongst His own. Later, the Temple succeeded the Tabernacle and once again 'the glory of the LORD ... filled the house of the LORD' (1 Kgs 8:1–11).

The descent of the glory of the LORD was the sign of God's dwelling, and without it the Temple was merely an ornate shell. And, tragically, the moment did come in the history of Israel when the glory departed, gradually, almost reluctantly, but unnoticed by the inhabitants of Jerusalem:

> Then the glory of the LORD went up from the cherub, and stood over the threshold of the house; and the house was filled with the cloud, and the court was full of the brightness of the LORD's glory (Ezek. 10:4)

> Then the glory of the LORD departed from off the threshold of the house, and stood over the cherubims. And the cherubims lifted up their wings, and mounted up from the earth in my sight: when they went out, the wheels also were beside them, and every one stood at the door of the east gate of the Lord's house; and the glory of the God of Israel was over them above (Ezek. 10:18–19).

Ultimately, the moment came when the prophecy of the Lord Jesus came to pass:

> Seest thou these great buildings? There shall not be left one stone upon another, that shall not be thrown down (Mk 13:2).

As the Roman legions stormed the defences of Jerusalem, these words were fulfilled with a terrible exactitude. On July 29, AD 70, flames engulfed Herod's Temple, and what the fire spared, looting legionaries soon destroyed. But the edifice that was reduced to ruins was no longer the House of God. That distinction had long since passed away from the sanctuary at Jerusalem.

Even when indwelt by the presence of God, however, the Tabernacle and the Temple were merely the 'example and shadow of heavenly things' (Heb.8:5), the 'pattern [figurative representations, *Darby*] of things in the heavenlies' (Heb. 9:23).

By contrast, in the dispensation of grace, we worship in 'a greater and more perfect tabernacle, not made with hands, that is to say, not of this building' (Heb. 9:11). We do not offer sacrifices at any earthly altar – at Shiloh, Jerusalem, or Mount Gerizim. Our feet tread the precincts of no mundane sanctuary. Our tabernacle is 'not of this building', it is spiritual and heavenly. It is the reality that was prefigured in the Tabernacle, the substance foreshadowed by the Temple.

This heavenly sanctuary is not the only dwelling place of God in this dispensation. The Lord Jesus promised 'I will build my Church; and the gates of hell shall not prevail against it' (Mt. 16:18) and Ephesians 2:19–22 identifies the type of building that is being constructed:

> Now therefore ye are no more strangers and foreigners, but fellowcitizens with the saints, and of the household of God; and are built upon the foundation of the apostles and prophets, Jesus Christ himself being the chief corner stone; in whom all the building fitly framed together groweth unto an holy temple in the Lord: in

Whom ye also are builded together for an habitation of God through the Spirit.

Believers in this dispensation 'are built up a spiritual house'. It is not the case, as with Israel, that the dwelling-place of God is in our midst. Rather, we are the dwelling place of God, His holy temple, His spiritual house.

The Church, the body of Christ, comprises every believer from Pentecost until the Rapture. Only a small fraction of this great mystical body is on Earth at any given time. But God does have an earthly dwelling place today – indeed, He has a multitude of them. Paul, with a note of incredulity and rebuke asked the Corinthians 'Know ye not that ye are the temple of God, and that the Spirit of God dwelleth in you?' (1 Cor. 3:16) and in his second letter reminded them that they were 'the temple of the living God' (2 Cor. 6:16). He emphasised to Timothy the vital importance of realising that the church of God – the company of believers gathered together in the name of the Lord Jesus Christ (Mt. 18:20) – is 'house of God'. The buildings in which we meet are not temples, but the remarkable truth of Scripture is that those who meet there, who gather in testimony to the Lord Jesus Christ are the earthly dwelling place of God, His abode, His holy place.

Perhaps more remarkable is the solemn yet stupendous truth that the bodies of individual believers are temples in which God dwells. Once again, Paul demanded of the Corinthians:

> What? know ye not that your body is the temple of the Holy Ghost which is in you, which ye have of God, and ye are not your own? For ye are bought with a price: therefore glorify God in your body, and in your spirit, which are God's (1 Cor. 6:15).

'AN HOLY PRIESTHOOD'

Like the Tabernacle, the Aaronic priesthood was central to the worship of the dispensation of Law:

> Now when these things were thus ordained, the priests went always into the first tabernacle, accomplishing the service of God. But into the second went the high priest alone once every year, not without blood, which he offered for himself, and for the errors of the people (Heb. 9:6–7)

The priests were responsible to 'accomplish the service of God', to offer the sacrifices that the Law required, and to carry out the ritual of the Temple. Their role was one of vital importance, and their position was highly privileged, but their character is tersely summed up by the writer to the Hebrews: 'the Law maketh men high priests which have infirmity' (Heb. 7:28). These priests were men, marked by sin, who 'were not suffered to continue by reason of death' (Heb. 7:23).

God had never intended the Aaronic priesthood to endure. It was temporary and provisional, pointing forward to a different order of priesthood and another – and infinitely greater – priest:

> If therefore perfection were by the Levitical priesthood, (for under it the people received the law,) what further need was there that another priest should rise after the order of Melchisedec, and not be called after the order of Aaron? (Heb. 7:11)

The other priest Who 'should' rise was superior in every way to the priests who served under the Levitical system:

> But this man, because He continueth ever, hath an unchangeable priesthood. Wherefore He is able also to save them to the uttermost that come unto

> God by Him, seeing He ever liveth to make intercession for them. For such an high Priest became us, Who is holy, harmless, undefiled, separate from sinners, and made higher than the heavens; Who needeth not daily, as those high priests, to offer up sacrifice, first for His own sins, and then for the people's: for this He did once, when He offered up Himself (Heb. 7:24-27).

The priesthood of the Lord Jesus Christ is greater because 'He continueth ever'. Death brought an end to the service of the sons of Aaron, they 'were not suffered to continue'. By contrast, our great high Priest 'ever liveth'. The moment will never come when He is obliged to abandon His ministry, or will cease to be our representative in the presence of God. As we have already seen, He is greater because of the sphere of His service. The earthly priest went into the Holiest of All once a year, bearing blood to cover his own sins, as well as those of the people. Our high Priest has been 'made higher than the heavens'. His ministry is carried out in 'heaven itself', where He appears 'in the presence of God for us' (Heb. 9:24).

Let us not miss the wonder of the high Priest that we have. To the empathy and understanding of the Aaronic priesthood, He adds the perfections of His sinless humanity. He represents us in the presence of God – appearing there 'for us'. And let us not overlook the almost incredible statement that 'such an high priest became us', that it was fitting that we should have a high Priest of this unique calibre and ability. How special we must be in the sight of God if He deems it appropriate that so great a priest should be ours. May we rejoice that we have 'such an high priest', and may we appreciate all that we owe to the ministry of the One Who is able to save us to the uttermost. 'And having an high priest over the house of God; Let us draw near with a true heart in full assurance of faith, having our hearts sprinkled from an evil conscience, and our bodies washed with pure water' (Heb. 10:21–22).

> *Before the throne of God above*
> *I have a strong and perfect plea.*
> *A great high Priest Whose name is Love*
> *Who ever lives and pleads for me.*
> *My name is graven on His hands,*
> *My name is written on His heart.*
> *I know that while in Heaven He stands*
> *No tongue can bid me thence depart.*
> —Charitie L. Bancroft

The Lord Jesus Christ, then, is our great high priest. In heaven, he exercises a spiritual ministry on our behalf. But His is not the only priesthood associated with this dispensation. His office as high priest is unique, but those who have believed on Him are also spoken of as a 'holy priesthood' (1 Pet.2:5) and 'a royal priesthood' (1 Pet. 2:9). The Apostle John opened the book of Revelation by speaking of 'the One Who loves us, and has washed us from our sins in His own blood, and hath made us a kingdom, priests to His God and Father. (Rev. 1:5–6, *Darby*), and those words will form part of our song as, in adoring worship, we gather round the throne of God and the Lamb (Rev. 5:10).

The privilege of being a holy nation and a kingdom of priests had been promised by God to the nation of Israel at the giving of the Law:

> Now therefore, if ye will obey My voice indeed, and keep My covenant, then ye shall be a peculiar treasure unto Me above all people: for all the earth is Mine: And ye shall be unto Me a kingdom of priests, and an holy nation (Exod. 19:5–6)

Israel's failure to keep the conditions of the Divine covenant meant that she never functioned as a kingdom of priests. Priesthood became limited to one family, and anyone who sought illegitimately to arrogate to himself the privileges of the priesthood faced terrible consequences (see, for example, the story of Uzziah in 2 Chron. 26:16–21). Direct access to the presence of God was limited to one man, once a year, while the congregation waited anxiously, outside the tent of meeting (Lev. 16:17).

How different is our position. We can 'draw near' to God. We 'come boldly unto the throne of grace' (Heb. 4:16). We enjoy the priesthood of all believers, and we should guard that privilege carefully. Down through the centuries, there have always been those whose ambition it has been to limit and curtail the priesthood of believers. We must be implacably opposed to any and every effort that seeks to rob us of our freedom to function as priests, publically or privately, in prayer, or praise, or worship. Rather, we should 'stand fast therefore in the liberty wherewith Christ hath made us free, and be not entangled again with the yoke of bondage' (Eph. 5:1), and rejoice in our spiritual liberty to function as priests in the sanctuary of our God.

'SPIRITUAL SACRIFICES'

The worship of God in the dispensation of Law involved a sanctuary – the Tabernacle or the Temple. It involved a priesthood – men who were specially appointed to represent the nation before God. And it required a third element, identified by the writer to the Hebrews:

> For every high priest is ordained to offer gifts and sacrifices: wherefore it is of necessity that this Man have somewhat also to offer (Heb. 8:3).

The work of the priests was intimately concerned with the preparation and offering of sacrifices. The burnt offering, the meal offering, the peace offering, the sin offering, and the trespass offering each had their varied requirements, but each required a priest to prepare the sacrifice, to place it upon the altar, to tend the flames that consumed it, and to remove the ashes that remained. Priests were busy men, who must have seldom have had empty hands.

With every other element of the Levitical system, these sacrifices were typical, pointing forward to the great sacrifice of the Lord Jesus Christ, and eloquently itemising the glorious significance of the 'one sacrifice for sin' (Heb. 10:12) that He would offer at Calvary. His sacrifice dealt with sin, and it delighted the heart of God, for He offered Himself 'an offering and a sacrifice to God for a sweetsmelling savour' (Eph. 5:2).

The sacrifice of the Lord Jesus Christ is supreme and solitary in its significance. No other sacrifice ever offered can be compared with that which was made when He 'through the eternal Spirit offered Himself without spot to God' (Heb. 9:14). But the New Testament also speaks of sacrifices that we can offer. Like the priests in the Temple, we too must have something to offer. And, just as the physical sacrifices of the Levitical order echoed and epitomised the physical nature of the system as a whole, so the character of our sacrifices is in keeping with the spiritual nature of our sanctuary and our priesthood:

> Ye also, as lively stones, are built up a spiritual house, an holy priesthood, to offer up spiritual sacrifices, acceptable to God by Jesus Christ (1 Pet 2:5).

The Levitical priesthood had a rich variety of sacrifices to offer. Similarly, the New Testament outlines the variety of sacrifice that we can offer. The writer to the Hebrews, for example, presents us with three different types of sacrifice that are wellpleasing to God:

> By him therefore let us offer the sacrifice of praise to God continually, that is, the fruit of our lips giving thanks to His name. But to do good and to communicate forget not: for with such sacrifices God is well pleased (Heb. 13:15–16).

Our praise – the 'fruit of our lips', our good deeds, and our material possessions are all presented as spiritual sacrifices in these verses. How this elevates and ennobles the mundane activities of our Christian lives. Putting our offering in the box, singing hymns, giving thanks, being kind to our neighbours are sacrifices that bring pleasure to God. Indeed, while the Apostle Paul spoke generally of the 'the sacrifice and service' of the Philippian believers' faith (Phil. 2:17) he singled out their material giving for special mention, describing it as 'an odour of a sweet smell, a sacrifice acceptable, wellpleasing to God' (Phil. 4:18).

The categories of spiritual sacrifice outlined in Hebrews 13 include a great deal of our lives. More comprehensive still is Paul's appeal in Romans 12:1:

> I beseech you therefore, brethren, by the mercies of God, that ye present your bodies a living sacrifice, holy, acceptable unto God, which is your reasonable service.

Here we are not contrasting physical sacrifices with spiritual, but a living sacrifice with dead sacrifices. God wants us to lay all that we are upon the altar for Him, to present our bodies, dedicating all that we are to His service. Worship in the Old Testament must frequently have been a costly business – it was no small thing to see a prime bullock go up in smoke. But even the most energetic giver fell short of what is our 'reasonable service'. It is God's desire that we hold nothing back, but offer all we are and have to Him, as the only logical response to the glory of His person and the greatness of His mercies.

Take my life, and let it be consecrated, Lord, to Thee.
Take my moments and my days; let them flow in ceaseless praise.
Take my hands, and let them move at the impulse of Thy love.
Take my feet, and let them be swift and beautiful for Thee.

Take my voice, and let me sing always, only, for my King.
Take my lips, and let them be filled with messages from Thee.
Take my silver and my gold; not a mite would I withhold.
Take my intellect, and use every power as Thou shalt choose.

Take my will, and make it Thine; it shall be no longer mine.
Take my heart, it is Thine own; it shall be Thy royal throne.
Take my love, my Lord, I pour at Thy feet its treasure store.
Take myself, and I will be ever, only, all for Thee.
–Francis Ridley Havergal

CHAPTER 4

WORSHIP AND ITS DIMENSIONS

FEW OF US would question the statement that the worship of God is the most important activity of our Christian lives. God desires it, Scripture exhorts it and the saints of old exemplify it. But as well as thinking about the importance of worship, we should think about the dimensions that it has, and that it should have in our lives.

In spite of the lip service that we play to the importance of worship, we seem, at times, to be in the grip of a tacit assumption that worship is a fairly confined business, expressed fully on a Lord's Day morning and then left to one side for another week. As with all our assumptions, we do well to test this idea by Scripture and, when we do so, we discover that worship has far more expansive dimensions than we might have imagined.

WORSHIPFUL WORK

Worship in Scripture can last for seconds. It can hardly have taken Mary more than that to utter the word 'Rabboni' when she recognised the Lord Jesus after His resurrection (Jn 20:16). Into that one word she packed a wealth of worship. On the other extreme, worship is seen as occupying a whole lifetime. So, in the opening verses of Romans 12, Paul follows the great doxology of chapter 11 with an exhortation for his readers to echo that worships with their own lives:

> I beseech you therefore, brethren, by the mercies of God, that ye present your bodies a living sacrifice, holy, acceptable unto God, which is your reasonable service ['spiritual worship' ESV] (Rom. 12:1).

The word translated as 'service' here involves more than the work of a servant. As the alternative translation indicates, this service has implicit in it the concept of worship. In this chapter, worship means far more than singing hymns and praying – it encompasses the transforming of our minds (v. 2), and the exercise of God-given gift. In the same way, the Lord Jesus brings the concepts of worship and service together when, in response to the temptation of Satan, He quotes Deuteronomy 6:13: 'Get thee hence, Satan: for it is written, Thou shalt worship the Lord thy God, and him only shalt thou serve' (Mt. 4:10).

Similarly, when Paul defended himself before Felix, he asserted the scriptural orthodoxy of his worship using the same word:

> But this I confess unto thee, that after the way which they call heresy, so worship I the God of my fathers, believing all things which are written in the law and in the prophets (Acts 24:14).

This reminds us that worship and service are not isolated concepts. Rather, true service for God, performed in communion with Him, and motivated by a sense of His greatness is worship. As such, our worship cannot be confined to an hour and a half on Lord's Day morning. It must permeate our lives and touch all that we do.

WORSHIPFUL WORKERS – ANNA

This becomes very clear when we trace the references to worshipful service through our New Testament. In doing so, we first encounter one of the attractive characters of Scripture. Anna 'was a widow of about fourscore and four years, which departed not from the temple, but served God with fastings and prayers night and day' (Lk. 2:37). There was nothing intermittent about Anna's worship – it was continuous and consistent and had occupied a lifetime of devotion to God. In her prayer life, that least spectacular and yet most vital component of Christian life, she was a faithful worshipper.

PAUL

The life of the Apostle Paul was marked by a similar consistency in worship. As he stood on the deck of the storm tossed ship to reassure his fellow travellers, he summed up his life in two simple clauses: 'God, whose I am, and whom I serve' (Acts 27:23). In the life of the Apostle, that worshipful service took a variety of forms. He reminded the Romans that his worship involved both his preaching and his prayer: 'For God is my witness, whom I serve with my spirit in the gospel of his Son, that without ceasing I make mention of you always in my prayers' (Rom. 1:9). While Paul's gospel was motivated by 'the terror of the Lord' and 'the love of Christ' (2 Cor. 5:11,14), and while he felt himself to be 'debtor both to the Greeks, and to the Barbarians; both to the wise, and to the unwise' (Rom. 1:14) his ministry in the gospel was also an ongoing act of worship, performed not half-heartedly but 'with [his] spirit'.

Writing to Timothy, he expressed a similar link between his worship and his prayer: 'I thank God, whom I serve from my forefathers with pure conscience, that without ceasing I have remembrance of thee in my prayers night and day' (2 Tim. 1:3).

THE PHILIPPIANS

Material giving is also included within the sphere of worship. In the epistle to the Philippians, Paul sees the Philippian believers and himself as united together in sacrificial worship: 'yea, and if I be offered upon the sacrifice and service of your faith, I joy, and rejoice with you all' (Phil. 2:17). In a humility that is entirely in keeping with his teaching earlier in chapter 2, Paul is happy to see his service as merely the drink offering poured out on the far more considerable and consequential offering of the Philippians. And he maintains this theme of worship into chapter 4, where he expresses his thankfulness for the gift that he had received from Philippi:

> But I have all, and abound: I am full, having received of Epaphroditus the things which were sent from you, an odour of a sweet smell, a sacrifice acceptable, wellpleasing to God (Phil. 4:18).

The Philippians' act of fellowship with the apostle – their practical desire to assist with his pecuniary needs – was more than a transfer of funds. It was an act of worship that delighted God.

ME?

This sort of worship is open to – and incumbent upon – us all. The writer to the Hebrews reminds us that we have been fitted for such worshipful service by 'the blood of Christ, who through the eternal Spirit offered himself without spot to God', which has the power to 'purge [our] conscience from dead works to serve the living God (Heb. 9:14). Later in the epistle he reminds us that our supreme blessing from God demands a diligent response to God:

> Wherefore we receiving a kingdom which cannot be moved, let us have grace, whereby we may serve God acceptably with reverence and godly fear (Heb. 12:28).

Worship is not something to be confined in any one compartment of our lives. Our appreciation of Who God is and of What He has and will do ought to affect everything that we undertake for God. Only this is a sufficient and a satisfactory motivation. Service that is simply routine, or grudgingly performed because it's our turn or something that is expected of us falls very far short of the Scriptural ideal. In the words of J.N. Darby:

> It is not service at all, if it be merely outward; unless we can say, 'Of Thine own we have given Thee.' All true service must flow from communion with the source of service; it is no service if we are not drinking in Christ, and conscious that we are doing His will; ... Service then, if real, must flow from direct communion with God.[*]

We serve and worship God now. The dimensions of that worship should be such as to leave no corner of our lives untouched, no moment of our time unaffected. We all fall far short of this ideal. Our

---

[*] J.N. Darby, *Collected Writings*, 26:28

worship is a niggardly business at best. Like the Hebrews, we need God's grace to serve Him acceptably. As we do so, let us encourage our hearts in the knowledge that one day soon our partial and imperfect worship will swell to fill an eternity of bliss. In the final reference to the service of worship in Scripture we have a most precious promise: 'and His servants shall serve Him: And they shall see His face; and His name shall be in their foreheads' (Rev. 22:3–4).

Chapter 5

Worship Directed

GOD CARES ABOUT the worship of His people. The elaborate directions for the tabernacle, the offerings and the feasts, given in the opening books of Scripture, are an ample testament to this fact. Nor do the change of dispensations and the dawning of the day of grace alter this fact. God still cares about worship, and it is still His desire that it be offered as He directs. His directions address every aspect of our worship, but most fundamentally of all, God's Word makes it clear Who the objects of our worship ought to be.

Misdirected Worship

Worship is always towards someone or something. Who or what we worship says a great deal about us. It ought to go without saying that the music and sports stars that provide the unsaved with their idols ought not to draw out any veneration from those who have known the 'only true God, and Jesus Christ, whom [He] sent' (Jn 17:3). The material objects that occupy our materialistic, possession-obsessed society should hold scant charm for those who have seen 'the glory of God in the face of Jesus Christ' (2 Cor. 4:6). Likewise, the worship of the body that has become the major religion in western society, at least, can hardly seem other than 'vanity and vexation of spirit' (Eccl. 1:14) to those who realise that it is 'the things that are not seen [that] are eternal' (2 Cor. 4:18).

What is, and what ought to be, are sometimes at variance, and we need to guard against succumbing to the lure of world-worship. We need, also, to be alert to the more insidious forms of misdirected worship. Peter disclaimed the worship of Cornelius with the words 'Stand up; I myself also am a man' (Acts 10:26), and John was rebuked for worshipping a servant of God – even an angelic one (Rev. 22:9). The brazen servant was manufactured by Divine command, and had been used of God in blessing His people. In spite of that, Hezekiah is commended for destroying it, and putting a stop to the idolatrous worship that was being offered to it (2 Kgs 18:34). Similarly, Gideon's ephod may well have been the fruit of a spiritual impulse, but it was nonetheless 'a snare unto Gideon, and to his house', and the object of idolatry as 'all Israel went thither a whoring after it' (Judg. 8:27). Even in spiritual things, especially in spiritual things, we need to be watchful lest our worship be diverted from the greater to the lesser good.

GOD-DIRECTED WORSHIP

Worship belongs exclusively to God. The opening words of the first table of the law leave little room for confusion:

> I am the LORD thy God, which have brought thee out of the land of Egypt, out of the house of bondage. Thou shalt have no other gods before Me. Thou shalt not make unto thee any graven image, or any likeness of any thing that is in heaven above, or that is in the earth beneath, or that is in the water under the earth: Thou shalt not

bow down thyself to them, nor serve them: for I the LORD thy God am a jealous God (Exod. 20:25).

The Lord Jesus, Himself, echoed these words when Satan promised Him the kingdoms of the Earth in exchange for His worship (Mt. 4:10, Lk. 4:8).

CHRIST-DIRECTED WORSHIP

As God, the Lord Jesus, too, should be the object of our worship. Scripture records that He received worship from the wise men (Mt. 2:2, 11), from a leper (Mt. 8:2), Jairus (Mt. 9:18), the women of Canaan (Mt. 15:25), the mother of James and John (Mt. 20:20), the blind man (Jn 9:38), His disciples (Mt. 14:3, 28:9, 17; Lk. 24:52), angels (Heb. 1:6, Rev. 5:11), the elders and the beasts (Rev. 4:9–11, Rev. 5:11–12). In a coming day, He will receive it from 'every creature which is in heaven, and on the earth, and under the earth, and such as are in the sea, and all that are in them' (Rev. 5:13) as 'at the name of Jesus every knee should bow, of things in heaven, and things in earth, and things under the earth; and ... every tongue confess that Jesus Christ is Lord, to the glory of God the Father' (Phil. 2:10–11).

There is, of course, no conflict between these incidents and God's commandment. Jesus Christ, the Lord is worthy of worship because He is Divine. He is 'the brightness of [God's] glory, and the express image of His person' (Heb. 1:3), the One Who is the eternal Word (Jn 1:1–14) Who declares the Father (Jn 1:18). As such, we see in Him every attribute of Deity perfectly displayed, and must, inevitably, respond with worship.

SPIRIT-DIRECTED WORSHIP?

We worship the Father and the Son. But what of the Holy Spirit? He too is Divine, part of the eternal Trinity. Are we not therefore to worship Him? A quick survey of much of the self-proclaimed worship in the world of contemporary evangelicalism would suggest that He is a major object of worship. By contrast, Scripture does not record a single incident where worship is directed to the Holy Spirit. This is not to deny His personality or His Deity – both are clearly taught in God's word. Rather, it reflects the self-effacing – though vital – nature of His ministry. Speaking of the Comforter Whom the Father would send, the Lord Jesus foretold that 'He shall testify of Me' (Jn 15:26). A little later, the Saviour expanded on the Spirit's ministry. In relation to the unregenerate 'He will reprove the world of sin, of righteousness, and of judgement' (Jn 16:8). In relation to the believer the Saviour promised:

> Howbeit when He, the Spirit of truth, is come, He will guide you into all truth: for He shall not speak of Himself; but whatsoever He shall hear, that shall He speak: and He will shew you things to come. He shall glorify Me: for He shall receive of Mine, and shall shew it unto you. All things that the Father hath are Mine: therefore said I, that He shall take of Mine, and shall shew it unto you (Jn 16:13–15).

It is the role of the Spirit, therefore, to glorify Christ. Like Abraham's servant, who so beautifully depicts the ministry of the Spirit in the present age (Gen. 24), He does not speak of Himself, but of the bridegroom. We cannot do without His ministry, and far too often we are impoverished in our understanding and appreciation of what He does for, in, and through us. We should thank God far more than we do for this Comforter Who is with us and in us. In spite of that, we should be very cautious about doing what Scripture neither mandates not records.

Worship that is not directed to the Godhead is idolatry. It is the ultimate debasement, a misappropriation of a capacity designed by God for God alone. The history of Israel demonstrates both the insidiousness allure of idolatry and its serious implications for the people of God. May God give us grace, in our day, to keep more faithfully the instruction of Moses: 'Thou shalt fear the LORD thy God; Him shalt thou serve, and to Him shalt thou cleave' (Deut. 10:20).

Chapter 6

Worship Delivered

THE ACCESSION TO the throne of Judah of King Hezekiah triggered one of the most radical reformations recorded in the Old Testament. Notwithstanding the darkness of prevailing conditions, Hezekiah's earnest exercise saw the nation's worship restored; delivered from the darkness and idolatry into which it had slipped.

Problems

Hezekiah faced formidable problems. 1 Kings 18:4 reveals the false worship that prevailed in Judah. The people worshipped in the high places and the groves, and had set up the brazen serpent as the object of idolatrous veneration. More poignant, still, perhaps, is the state of the temple (2 Chron. 29:7). Its doors, which should have stood open to admit the worship of God's people, were tightly shut. Dust and dirt filled its holy compartments. The lamps had been extinguished and the altars, which should have been continuously occupied with sacrifices, stood empty and deserted.

Beyond question, these were dark days of dearth and departure. What about our day? Are our lamps dim or extinguished, and are our altars dusty through disuse? Is the energy that should be directed to the worship of our God being dissipated in other places and other pursuits? Do we, too, need a God-given deliverance of our worship from the bondage of barrenness and the durance of dearth?

Priority

When Hezekiah became king, there were urgent matters that called for his attention. It is clear from 2 Chronicles 32 that the defences of Jerusalem, in particular, required attention. We might well have expected that it would be this task of fortification that would have been at the top of the new king's to-do list, that the renewing the city's defences would have had the highest priority.

For Hezekiah, however, the true source of security and safety did not lie in walls or in feats of engineering. With spiritual discernment, he was able to identify the most pressing need. It was 'in the first year of his reign, in the first month' (2 Chron. 29:3) that he initiated his programme of reform.

We need to ask ourselves how our priorities compare with Hezekiah's. We would all like to be stronger in testimony for God than we are. In this endeavour, walls and defences have a vital part to play. But however important, they are not the most fundamental things. Worship is both the source and the measure of our strength. If we get it wrong, it really doesn't matter what else we get right. May God give us the understanding that Hezekiah had, and cause us to appreciate that it is a weakness in worship, above all else that constrains our testimony and curtails our power.

Pattern

Hezekiah faced a difficult – even dire – situation. Worship was not working, and something clearly needed to be done. If many of us encountered similar circumstances, our impulse would be to innovate. Clearly, we would reason, the old pattern does not work: we need something new. There is no indication that Hezekiah was tempted to implement a novel solution. He understood that the problems affecting the worship of God did not stem from a problem with the pattern. Rather, the great difficulty was a failure faithfully to follow the pattern provided by God's Word. This was a reformation and a revival – Hezekiah went back to worship 'of such sort as it was written' (2 Chron. 30:5).

The restored worship took its pattern from Divine revelation. It was from this source too that it drew its praise:

> Moreover Hezekiah the king and the princes commanded the Levites to sing praise unto the Lord with the words of David, and of Asaph the seer' (2 Chron. 29:30).

The form and content of worship had already been provided; what was needed was not innovation or modification, but faithfulness to the Word of God.

This lesson is vital for us. We will never encounter circumstances that justify abandoning the Divine pattern. We live in days when a whole array of cacophonous expedients have been added to or have replaced the simplicity of scriptural, spiritual worship. It is easy for us to stray from God's pattern. Whether that movement is sudden and startling or gradual and incremental makes no difference to its seriousness. In our collective worship we will never improve on the sacredness of the upper room, nor should we desire to. 'When the hour was come, he sat down, and the twelve apostles with Him' (Lk. 22:14), and no innovation will ever compensate for His absence.

PEOPLE

The deliverance of worship began with an exercise in the heart of King Hezekiah. It did not stop there, but spread in expanding ripples to touch many of God's people. After the king, it touched the priests and the Levites. Hezekiah reminded them of their privilege and responsibility:

> My sons, be not now negligent: for the LORD hath chosen you to stand before him, to serve him, and that ye should minister unto him, and burn incense (2 Chron. 29:11).

It seems that they needed this reminder. They had lost sight of their remarkable calling to be worshippers of God. Only when they regained an appreciation of this were they ready to begin again the work of worship. We, too, have a high calling. From us, the Father seeks worship in spirit and in truth (Jn 4:24). If we only grasped the dignity and the privilege of this calling we, like the Levites and priests, would be ashamed at the way in which we have been in dereliction of our duty of worship.

Revival had to spread further still. That it did so indicated clearly the Divine source of this reformation: 'And Hezekiah rejoiced, and all the people, that God had prepared the people: for the thing was done suddenly' (2 Chron. 29:26). And there was no shortage of tangible evidence that the hearts of God's people had been touched. They brought their offerings to the temple in such profusion that 'the priests were too few, so that they could not flay all the burnt offerings' (2 Chron. 29:34). In contrast to the days of empty altars and dusty courts, there was now an overflowing of worship.

We would love to know something of this. For our worship to overflow the available time and resources would be a wonderful – and a sadly unusual – thing. The events of this revival prove that it is possible. But it is only possible if the hearts of individual believers are touched, and the souls of God's people exercised to sacrifice. Only thus can a revival of worship be known. It cannot be achieved by importing 'worship leaders'; it cannot be stirred up by individual charisma or by any other means. It can only stem from the commitment of individual believers before God.

It is encouraging to note that the effects of this revival spread still further. In chapter 30, the posts go out with words of invitation – and of warning:

> Ye children of Israel, turn again unto the LORD God of Abraham, Isaac, and Israel, and he will return to the remnant of you ... Now be ye not stiffnecked, as your fathers were, but yield yourselves unto the LORD, and enter into his sanctuary, which he hath sanctified for ever: and serve the LORD your God. (2 Chron. 30:6–8)

The message reveals a longing that God's people would be united in worship, but it also reveals a clear understanding that such unity could not be purchased at the price of compromise.

PLACE

In Hezekiah's letter we see an insistence on the importance of scriptural pattern and place in the carrying out of worship. All Israel and Judah (2 Chron. 30:6) were welcome to worship God, but they must do it in His way, at His place, and in a spirit of repentance. To a Godless man like Sennacherib, this seemed arrogance of the highest order:

> Hath not the same Hezekiah taken away his high places and his altars, and commanded Judah and Jerusalem, saying, Ye shall worship before one altar, and burn incense upon it? (32:12).

In reality, though, Hezekiah was not motivated by arrogance or presumption but by his faithfulness to the Word of God.

In this dispensation of grace we are not geographically limited in our worship (Jn 4:21). Individually, we can worship God, no matter where we are. But we do well to remember that there is still a place that is described as 'the temple of the living God' (2 Cor. 6:16). The local church is the Divinely-mandated place where our collective worship and service is to be offered, and what we offer anywhere else is less than it should be.

Like Hezekiah, we desire that all God's people would be united in worship. But we should appreciate, as he did, that such a unity can only be based on submission to the Word of God. Such an attitude, now as then, is sometimes dismissed as arrogance, and there is an ever-present danger of slipping into such a loathsome state of mind. But this should not make us less determined to insist – humbly but firmly – on the absolute importance of obedience to the Word of God, and the Divine pattern of gathering that it contains.

Prosperity

The results of delivered worship are predictable, but nonetheless remarkable. With God receiving His rightful portion 'there was great joy in Jerusalem: for since the time of Solomon the son of David king of Israel there was not the like in Jerusalem' (2 Chron. 30:26). Along with that joy came an abundance of blessing, well beyond what was required:

> Since the people began to bring the offerings into the house of the LORD, we have had enough to eat, and have left plenty: for the LORD hath blessed his people; and that which is left is this great store (31:10).

The exercise of a Godly king had delivered the worship of God's people from darkness and dearth. His desire to worship found an answer in the hearts of the people. God was glorified, and His people blessed. There is much in the revival of Hezekiah's day to encourage and exhort us in the difficulties of our own day.

CHAPTER 7

WORSHIP DISPLAYED

BALAAM, THE RENEGADE PROPHET stood with Balak, king of Midian on the top of Mount Peor. This was his third attempt to curse Israel, and earn the generous reward promised by the king. Seven altars had been built, seven bullocks and seven rams slaughtered and sacrificed. Now Balaam stood, looking over the encamped nation spread on the face of the wilderness. With bated breath Balak waited to hear whether now, at last, this nation would be cursed. But when the prophet's words broke the silence, it was not to curse, but once again to bless: 'How goodly are thy tents, O Jacob, and thy tabernacles, O Israel!' (Num. 24:5).

The Israelite encampment must, undoubtedly, have been an impressive sight, with each tribe gathered in orderly array beneath their furling pennants. But one tent stood out above all others. Partly it owed its prominence to its size – it was considerably larger than the other tents. Partly too its location focused attention upon it – it lay at the centre of the camp. But mostly it attracted the viewer's eye because above it rested the pillar of cloud, the visible manifestation of God's presence with and protection of His chosen people.*

The tabernacle was a remarkable structure, but its significance was far more than architectural. It was God's earthly dwelling place, the singular location ordained by God for His service. The tabernacle, and later the temple, were, in a unique way, places of worship, and their importance can be gauged by the number of pages of the Bible devoted to describing the details of their construction, and of the service to be carried on within their precincts. And, though the temple and the tabernacle no longer exist, and though priests no longer stand ministering in their courts, those passages are neither irrelevant nor redundant. Indeed, it is only in the light of the New Testament that we are able fully to understand the significance of the tabernacle. So, we learn that it is 'the example and shadow of heavenly things' (Heb. 8:5), 'the patterns of things in the heavens' (Heb. 9:23). That is, they present to us earthly and physical pictures of heavenly and spiritual truth. Preeminently, they speak to us of Christ. It is a fitting reflection of the infinite glory of His person and the fathomless greatness of His work that the tabernacle and the offerings in all their detail and variety serve only as a shadow, a partial and provisional symbol of a perfect and permanent reality.

But the tabernacle also tells us something about the service of God. In this dispensation, it is true, we do not serve a physical altar, or offer animal sacrifices. But nonetheless, the tabernacle does embody for our edification some important principles that are

---

* It is interesting to note that these lines from Balaam's prophecy are linked especially with the tabernacle in the *ma tovu*, a Jewish prayer that begins with this quotation and which is prayed when entering a synagogue. The remainder of the prayer is made up of quotations from Psalms 5:8; 26:8; 95:6; and 69:14.

enduringly important and relevant. This is clearly demonstrated by the writer to the Hebrews. Throughout his epistle, he has presented an unparalleled account of the typical significance of the tabernacle. As he draws the epistle to a close he indicates the relevance of the tabernacle as a practical example to those who worship God today:

> By Him therefore let us offer the sacrifice of praise to God continually, that is, the fruit of our lips giving thanks unto His name (Heb. 13:15).

Following the writer's example, there are a number of important principles connected with worship that we can learn from the tabernacle and its service.

PLACE OF WORSHIP

As Balaam and Balak looked over the camp of Israel, they had no difficulty in recognising the importance that the tabernacle and its service had for the life of the nation. The tabernacle was not tucked away in some obscure corner, or squeezed into the space left between the other tents. Rather, the tabernacle was located at the centre of the camp, and all the other tents were located by reference to the tabernacle:

> And the Lord spake unto Moses and unto Aaron, saying, Every man of the children of Israel shall pitch by his own standard, with the ensign of their father's house: far off about the tabernacle of the congregation shall they pitch (Num. 2:1–2).

God's tent had to be erected first: only when it stood in its proper place could the other tents be properly placed. Concern for the strategic arrangement of the camp or the whims and preferences of individual Israelites played no role in the organisation of the life of the nation: all the everyday details of life were ordered so that the service of God was central. The physical layout of the camp illustrated and affirmed the centrality of worship in the life of the nation. Worshiping God took precedence above everything else.

What was true of the nation in the wilderness should be true, too, of every believer in this dispensation. Our worship and our service for God should occupy the central place in our lives. It should be the first thing to be put in place, and all the other elements of our life – family, work, and leisure – ought to secondary. All too often we fail here. We lay out all the other tents that are so important in our busy lives, and then we shoehorn our worship into whatever meagre and misshapen plot remains. Rather than the disciplined order that wrung unwilling words of blessing from Balaam, the Peor-top view of our lives too often reveals a jumbled and dishevelled disarray. May God grant us His grace that we, with confession of our failure, might ensure that worship and service are restored to their proper and preeminent position in our lives.

'Giving worship first place in our lives' sounds rather vague and aspirational. In reality, however, it is as practical a matter for us as it was for the Israelites. They put up the tabernacle first, and everything else slotted into place around it. As we arrange our lives, and juggle with increasingly busy schedules, we need to make sure that it is spiritual activity that takes priority. This means arranging our lives to be able to attend the gatherings of the assembly. It means that time to read and pray should be a non-negotiable element of our daily diary. It means that we ensure that God gets His portion, in spite of the imperatives to 'work hard, play hard' that the world, our employers, colleagues, and friends seek to impress upon us.

PRECISION OF WORSHIP

The tabernacle drew the eyes of the onlookers on Peor. If the day was clear enough, and their eyesight sharp enough, they may well have been able to make out the forms of the priest moving to-and-fro in the court of the tabernacle. Their actions can only have made the scene more impressive. They moved with dignity in the service of God. Their steps were marked by reverent care, but also by the resolute confidence that came from knowing their role and their responsibilities. These priests were not improvising, but moving in scrupulous obedience to God's commands.

One of the most striking things about the tabernacle and its service is the tremendous wealth of detail provided by God in the instructions He gives. Some fifty chapters of the Bible are devoted to these directions – a marked contrast with the two that record the events of the creation. But it is not just the amount of instructions that is striking. Their detail and specificity is also remarkable. No detail of tabernacle service was so minute or so recondite as to escape mention. And these details are not optional possibilities. The word 'command' or its variants occur over one hundred times in Exodus and Leviticus, and on forty occasions the phrase 'as the Lord commanded Moses' occurs in connection with the ordering of the tabernacle. Furthermore, even beyond the detail that is directly recorded in Scripture, Moses' responsibility faithfully to implement the pattern that was shown to him on the summit of Sinai is clearly stressed in Exodus and, in Hebrews, he is explicitly commended for his faithfulness in relation to the house of God:

> According to all that I shew thee, after the pattern of the tabernacle, and the pattern of all the

> instruments thereof, even so shall ye make it (Exod. 25:9).
>
> And look that thou make them after their pattern, which was shewed thee in the mount (Exod. 25:40).
>
> Moses was faithful in all His house. And Moses verily was faithful in all His house, as a servant, for a testimony of those things which were to be spoken after (Heb. 3:3, 5).

It is very clear, then, that God's instructions about the tabernacle were marked by an exact and exacting precision. The tabernacle was not a place where anything went. Its order and service were not directed by human whim or by considerations of expediency. God gave the pattern, and it was man's responsibility to see that they followed it.

This precision mattered, because the tabernacle was to speak of Christ. It was to represent His character and His work, and thus it was vital that every detail be exactly right, so that God's great illustration would not be blurred or marred. But it also reminds us that the worship of God is not something to be carried out haphazardly or carelessly. God desires our worship to be real – He seeks worship 'in spirit' (Jn 4:24). He also desires our worship to be orderly and accurate – that we worship 'in truth'. He looks for passion in our worship, but it is a passionate precision that He seeks. And that precision comes not from the formularies or liturgies of men, but from the pages of His Word. There we learn Who we worship, and how we may be able to offer informed and intelligent adoration to our God. There, too, we learn the vital truths of where and how we worship.

The point made in a previous chapter deserves restatement here. Sincerity and spontaneity are neither exclusive of nor inimical to care, accuracy, and – again the word seems best – precision. The antics of emotionalism and the improvisations of the sensationalist are a very poor substitute for a dignified and decent worship that is engendered by meditation on the Word of God. Our worship as individuals, and collectively as companies of God's people should reflect our realisation that worship is a serious matter, about which God cares very deeply. Grasping this truth would cause us to move in His worship with the caution and yet with the confidence that so impressed Balaam as he gazed upon the goodly tents of Israel.

PRIORITY OF WORSHIP

The view from Peor was, of course, an unusual one. From a less elevated perspective, the white linen curtains that stood over seven feet tall around the perimeter of the tabernacle would have made it difficult to see much of what took place within. Even from a higher elevation, much of the tabernacle – and all of its most beautiful and intricate detail – remained concealed from the eyes of any but the priests. For the most part, they could not see the detail of the most ornate compartment, and even the high priest who was privileged to enter the holy of holies once a year (Heb. 9:7) would have seen little of its glories through the swirling clouds of incense even if the awful solemnity of the occasion had not made it utterly unsuitable for sightseeing (Lev. 16:12–13).

It may appear a strange thing that the beauty of the tabernacle should be thus concealed beneath drab exterior coverings. Given the costliness of the materials contributed by the people and the effort they invested in the equipping of the tent (Exod. 36:3–7), it seems hardly fair that they should be denied the opportunity to enjoy the opulence and splendour of the tabernacle.

Their lack of access strikes us as more surprising when we recall that on five occasions in Scripture the tabernacle is referred to as the tabernacle of witness (Num. 17:7-8; 18:2; 2 Chron. 24:6; Acts 7:44). The Hebrew word translated as 'witness' is also translated as 'testimony' and it has the sense of revealing or displaying something, and we use the word in this way when we speak of the testimony of an individual or an assembly before the unsaved – the way in which they are seen, the character that they reveal. We are accustomed to think of witness or testimony as being directed at our fellow men. So, as we think of the tabernacle as a 'tabernacle of witness' we might think of what it revealed to those like Balak and Balaam, who were not part of the nation, but who encountered God's people in their wilderness wanderings. Or we might think too of the tabernacle's testimony to the Israelites, of the wealth of spiritual truth that it daily presented to them. And both of these aspects are undoubtedly important. But it is also important that we remember that the tabernacle's testimony was directed primarily at the One Who alone was able to see all its beauty and appreciate all its significance. While the tabernacle was a witness to the Israelites and to the nations it was primarily for the eye of God.

This is a point of crucial importance and a slight digression is justified to underline its significance for our understanding of assembly testimony. When we think of our witness as churches of God, we often think of our testimony to the unsaved round about. For some, it is this aspect of testimony that takes priority, and so they speak of the need to become 'seeker-friendly' churches. Others see the assembly as being primarily for the benefit – and even for the comfort – of God's people. Neither of these views is entirely without validity. The assembly should be a testimony to the unsaved. The unsaved should be made welcome in our gatherings, and good it would be if the conduct of our meetings forced them to 'report that God is in [us] of a truth' (1 Cor. 14:25). It is also true that the assembly should be a place where God's people are fed and instructed. Beyond this, scriptural order in the church of God is a witness even to the angels (1 Cor. 11:10). But we must not allow ourselves to forget that the assembly is primarily for God, and that its most fundamental responsibility is to bring pleasure to Him.

And what is true of our testimony should also be true of our worship. Our public worship should be a blessing to the saints. It should also be a voice to any unsaved who may be listening. But if I get to my feet with any intention in my heart other than offering worship to God, I had far better stay seated. If I take part in public worship in order to impress my brethren or, even more reprehensibly, to take a swipe at them, I am betraying a sadly deficient understanding of the solemnity of worship. And, even though the sudden proliferation of prayers quoting John 3:16 that can arise when a stranger wanders into our gathering is prompted by the most laudable of evangelical motives, it is nonetheless a misuse of worship and a robbing of God. Let us ever be mindful that our worship is for God before anyone else. Let us remember that it is our unspeakable privilege to present Christ to God, and to gladden the heart of the Father by speaking well of His Son. And let us make sure that our worship is not a performance, limited to our public participation at the breaking of bread, but rather let us spend time in the inner sanctuary, giving God our worship.

POWER FOR WORSHIP

When Balaam exclaimed from the top of Peor he spoke of the tents of Israel. And that term is used in relation to the tabernacle as a whole (Exod. 39:32,40; 40:2,6; Num. 9:15), and in relation to its constituent compartments (Exod. 26:11–14, 36; 35:11; 36:14, 18–19). When we think of the tabernacle, we are reminded that this structure was the dwelling-place of God, where He was pleased to dwell in the midst of His people. When we think of it as a tent we are reminded of the nature of structure, of its tangible physical existence.

The tabernacle was a physical structure and the worship that was carried out there was, likewise, physical in its nature. Unlike the worship that characterises the present dispensation, the service of God in the tabernacle featured music, incense, and animal sacrifices. It was a tangible worship that involved all of the senses.

Notwithstanding this, it is important that we note that even this worship – so overtly physical in its nature – required spiritual power. The spiritual aspect of the tabernacle is perhaps nowhere so clear as in the account of its construction. Exodus 35 makes it very clear that the work of the Holy Spirit was vital in the manufacture of this remarkable tent.

The Spirit was active when it came to the contribution of materials for the tabernacle. Speaking to the Israelites Moses did not announce a command but an invitation:

> And Moses spake unto all the congregation of the children of Israel, saying, This is the thing which the LORD commanded, saying, Take ye from among you an offering unto the Lord: whosoever is of a willing heart, let him bring it, an offering of the LORD. (Exod. 35:4–5)

The Israelites responded to the invitation. Those who brought their goods as an offering were marked by two features:

> And they came, every one whose heart stirred him up, and every one whom His Spirit made willing, and they brought the LORD'S offering to the work of the tabernacle of the congregation, and for all His service, and for the holy garments. (v. 21)

Firstly, these individuals had stirred up their own hearts. They had within themselves a yearning to give, to bring something of value – and of cost to themselves – that would make a vital contribution – whether small or large – to the worship of God and the splendour of His dwelling place. This desire was inextricably linked to a spiritual exercise, to the work of the Holy Spirit Himself. What a pattern we have here for our own worship. We cannot worship acceptably apart from the power of the Holy Spirit, and His work in our hearts. But the Spirit does not take up unwilling or resisting instruments. Our own hearts must stir us up, and we must have the desire to worship, and a willingness to make costly sacrifices in order to express our appreciation of the glory and greatness of God.

The work of the Spirit did not end when the people had brought 'much more than enough for the service of the work' (Exod. 36:5). His ministry was needed as the design given to Moses was executed:

> And Moses said unto the children of Israel, See, the LORD hath called by name Bezaleel the son of Uri, the son of Hur, of the tribe of Judah; And He hath filled him with the Spirit of God, in wisdom, in understanding, and in knowledge, and in all manner of workmanship; And to devise curious works, to work in gold, and in silver, and in brass,

> And in the cutting of stones, to set them, and in carving of wood, to make any manner of cunning work. And He hath put in his heart that he may teach, both he, and Aholiab, the son of Ahisamach, of the tribe of Dan. Them hath He filled with wisdom of heart, to work all manner of work, of the engraver, and of the cunning workman, and of the embroiderer, in blue, and in purple, in scarlet, and in fine linen, and of the weaver, even of them that do any work, and of those that devise cunning work (Exod. 35:30–5).

The Israelites had been first farmers and then slaves in Egypt. When it came to building with brick, they were expert. Their arduous training under the lash of the taskmasters' whips meant that they were proficient in all the stages of building:

> And they built for Pharaoh treasure cities, Pithom and Raamses. ... And they made their lives bitter with hard bondage, in morter, and in brick, and in all manner of service in the field (Exod. 1:11, 14).

But God does not call upon any of that hard-bought knowledge. Rather, He commissions a tent; a structure that included all variety of highly skilled metal work, weaving, tapestry, and carving, but not a single brick. God is not interested in the skills that were so important in Egypt, but in those that the Spirit would teach, equipping men to make precisely the right contribution to the house of God.

Again, the application to testimony in the church age is obvious. In the assembly, God equips men to discharge a variety of tasks, and He does so without depending upon their natural talents or abilities. But the more specific application to our worship is also valid and helpful. Worship requires more than an eloquent tongue, a good memory for poetry, or a facility for striking imagery. True worship is spiritual in its energy. As King David realised on a very similar occasion, as the people offered for the construction of the temple, even as our worship rises to its highest heights, we can only offer back to God what we have received from Him in the first place:

> O LORD our God, all this store that we have prepared to build Thee an house for Thine holy name cometh of Thine hand, and is all Thine own. (1 Chron. 29:16)

Whether we think of material sacrifice (a vital part of our worship) or of the sacrifice of our time to learn more of God, or of the private or public worship we offer verbally to God, whatever it is, we are only giving Him what He has given us, and it is grace beyond our imagining that He values and rewards such offering.

The tabernacle must surely have made a profound impression upon Balaam and Balak as it stood shining in the shimmering heat of the wilderness. It was, indeed, a 'goodly tent' that lay before him, at the heart of the orderly ranks of tents that lay before him. We have never had the privilege to behold that magnificent vista but, with the benefit of scriptural spectacles we can see wealth of truth illustrated in the tabernacle. The tabernacle has much to teach us about Christ, about heaven, and about the service of God. And it has much to teach us about worship. In this chapter we have sought to learn some of the most important lessons that it has for us. As we meditate on this great object lesson in worship in the wilderness, provided by God Himself, may the truth that it exemplifies and expounds shape our service and deepen our worship for the glory of God, and for our own eternal blessing.

CHAPTER 8

WORSHIP DEPICTED

IN MATTHEW 26 the Lord Jesus Christ made a unique promise. This promise was not made to one of the disciples who followed Him throughout His ministry, nor to any of the prominent and important individuals with whom He had come into contact. Rather it was to a devoted woman that the Saviour made an unprecedented commitment:

> Verily I say unto you, Wheresoever this gospel shall be preached in the whole world, there shall also this, that this woman hath done, be told for a memorial of her (v. 13).

The action singled out for posterity by the Saviour is among the most precious and profound recorded in the gospels. Here was a woman, a sinner reached by the grace of God, whose appreciation of the Saviour poured out in an act of worship that has a great deal to teach us.

COSTLINESS

The most outstanding feature of this woman's deed – both to the disciples and to us – was its costliness. The ointment that she poured upon the Saviour was precious. Sold, it would have yielded much. As such it represented a considerable financial sacrifice. But it also embodied months, perhaps years, of self-denial, as this woman went without all manner of luxuries – and perhaps of necessities – in order that she might have something to pour out upon her Lord. In the calculations of the world, this was a waste. She could have enjoyed spending the money on herself, or could have prudently saved it against her future need. If she was set on sacrificing it, she could have expended it in practical charity. Anything, surely, would have been better than the wanton waste of unrestrainedly pouring out valuable ointment. But this woman evaluated the matter differently. The privilege of anointing her Saviour was well worth all that she had given up. In this estimation of the worth of the Lord she stands in stark contrast to Judas who, just verses later, placed the meagre value of thirty pieces of silver on the Christ of God. And the Saviour shared her spiritual economics. He knew exactly what it had cost her, and His response was measured by the value that He placed on her simple but profound act of devotion.

The woman's action reveals priorities that ought to challenge and humble us. As we gather to remember the Lord do we bring that which has been costly? Does our worship – silent or audible, from sister or brother – represent any real sacrifice on our part? Or, are we in danger of doing what David disclaimed: 'neither will I offer burnt offerings unto the LORD my God of that which doth cost me nothing' (2 Sam. 24:24). The action of this godly sister, so appreciated by the Saviour, though so little valued by others, should spur us to invest more seriously in our highest calling – to worship Him.

Considered

If the Saviour appreciated the value of the woman's offering, He noted too the consideration that it indicated. Her investment was not expended in a random act of impulse. This anointing was the act of an intelligent worshipper. She poured the ointment on Him for His burial (Mt. 26:12). In the careful precision of her action she displayed a spiritual discernment to which the disciples seemed unable to attain. This consideration in no way compromised the warmth and sincerity of her act; it immeasurably enhanced its worth.

We should aspire to worship like this. Our worship should display an intelligent appreciation of the nature of God and of the person of Christ. It should not only be doctrinally accurate; it should be saturated in Scripture. In spite of a prevailing mind-set that prizes spontaneity and informality and that creates a false opposition between the mind and the affections, this by no means implies that we should be stilted or artificial in our worship. Worship, to conform to the Scriptural ideal, must involve our hearts and our minds, our intellect and our affections. Like this woman, we enhance the beauty and value of our worship when we worship both in spirit and in truth.

Complete

It is significant that Matthew so carefully specifies the container in which this woman brought her ointment. The alabaster box must have been costly in itself, and beautiful in its craftsmanship and execution. But more importantly, it was a vessel that had to be broken. She did not bring a bottle or a flask that could have been stoppered up before all the ointment had poured out, allowing some of the precious cargo to be saved for later use. This worshipper holds nothing back, retains nothing. The box was broken, every last drop of the fragrance was liberated – reservation and reuse was not an option.

One of the greatest challenges that we face is maintaining freshness in our worship. Far too often we seem to come with a bottle, pouring out a niggardly measure of worship and then replacing the cork until the next Lord's Day arrives. Like the indolent Israelites, we have only worm-ridden and stinking manna. In view of the infinite and inexhaustible glories of the Person Who we worship, it is surely an incongruous thing if we constantly cover the same ground, using phrases so well worn that our fellow believers could almost recite them along with us. It would be more fitting if we had a fresh and fragrant appreciation of the Saviour to pour out without reservation upon His lovely person.

Consequences

This woman's act was attended by a number of consequences. It is precious to reflect that, as the Saviour left the house, He carried with Him a fragrance that would linger to Calvary and beyond. Even as the soldiers spat in His face they would have caught the aroma of this woman's devotion. As He hung on the cross, as He lay in the tomb, still there would linger the fragrance of worship. The woman's act glorified Christ, and we, too, can have no higher ambition for our worship.

The consequences did not stop there. As the fragrance of the ointment percolated through the room it would have clung to the woman's own clothing and to that of the disciples. Both the one who worshipped and those who looked on went on their way more fragrant, more obviously linked to Christ as a result of this worship.

Is our worship fragrant? We can add nothing intrinsic to Christ, but is there a portion for Him in our worship? Do we magnify His person, make His worth more evident? And what effect does our worship have on our fellow believers? Do they rise from the Lord's Table a little more fragrant, a little more like Christ because of my worship? This is what we should desire, for this is what true worship will accomplish.

And, as we have seen, there was another consequence of the woman's worship. The Saviour publically recorded His appreciation of the woman's act, and decreed that it would be remembered through centuries after. In a sense, the fragrance of her offering has never faded – it comes to us today just as sweet, just as sacred, and just as precious as it did in the house of Simon the leper.

As far as earth is concerned, no-one gets much recognition for worship. We have much to say about gift (and those who possess it) in relation to preaching and teaching. Very seldom is exercise in worship singled out for praise, or even for comment. And yet, it is the highest and most important form of service to which we can aspire. And it is recognised and rightly evaluated in the records of heaven.

The woman brought a costly offering but the consequences of her action and her compensation far outweighed any cost. In this she exemplifies for us the blessedness and the value of fulfilling our calling to be worshippers of our God.

Chapter 9

Worship Developed

In the preceding chapters of this book, we have considered various aspects of the subject of worship. We have looked at examples of worship from the Old Testament and the New, and have noted some important principles concerning the way in which God is to be worshipped. Perhaps the most important lesson that we can learn about worship is its fundamental importance. On this, the testimony of Scripture is clear – worship matters to God. And, because it matters to God, it must matter to us too. Because He values worship, so must we. Because He desires our worship, it must be our desire to offer what He seeks, and to delight God by our worship.

We would all like to be better worshippers. We long that our capacity and ability to worship might be deepened and developed. There is no easy way to achieve this, no book that we can read, no correspondence course that we can take. But, by God's grace, we can develop as worshippers. This chapter will outline some important principles and attempt to offer some practical suggestions to help us in that development.

THE RESPONSIBILITY OF WORSHIP

It is important to note, first of all, that worship is expected of each believer. Romans 12, 1 Corinthians 12, Ephesians 4, and 1 Peter 4 each contains lists of the gifts of the Spirit. Young believers are rightly exercised about identifying what their gift is, and we should all take care to be diligent in the exercise of our particular gift, 'to stir up the gift that is in you' (2 Tim. 1:6). Conversely, we should be very cautious about taking on activities for which we have not been gifted, for our lack of adeptness will be both obvious and burdensome to others. It is striking, however, that prayer does not appear on any of these lists. It does not appear, because prayer is the responsibility of every believer, and is, indeed, the inevitable consequence of our salvation (Rom. 8:15). And the same is true of worship. We cannot evade our responsibility by saying that we have no gift for worship. Every believer in the Lord Jesus Christ is expected *ipso facto* to be a worshipper.

Age and experience are not prerequisites for worship. The gospel records of those who were blessed by Christ make it clear that worship is the expected response from a new convert. Indeed, there is often a particular freshness and sweetness in the worship of a new believer, who is just beginning to grasp the greatness of God, of Christ and of salvation.

The New Testament makes it clear that sisters are 'silent in the church', and submission to Scriptural order means that women do not worship audibly. But that is very far from saying that they do not worship. In Anna (Lk. 2:36–8), in Mary (Jn 12:3), in the widow who gave all she had (Mk. 12:41–4), and in the women who so willingly offered their precious possessions for the construction of the tabernacle (Exod. 36:3–7), we have lovely examples of the value that God attaches to the worship of women.

Scripture neither contemplates nor countenances such a thing as an unworshipping believer. We can be clear and categorical about this – if we are saved, we must be worshippers. It matters not whether we be male or female – we must be worshippers. It matters not how young or how old we are – we must be worshippers. It matters not how busy our day, how heavy our responsibilities, or how full our time – we must worship, for God desires it and deserves it. In light of the greatness of His person, and the immensity and impact of what He has done for us, it is surely to our shame that our cold hearts and constrained spirits are so conspicuously costive in our response to Him.

Oh wonder to myself I am,
Thou loving, bleeding, suffering Lamb
That I can scan the mystery o'er
And not be moved to love Thee more!

Oh, I am weary of such love,
That doth so little toward Thee move;
Yet do I constantly, inly groan
To know the depths of all Thine own.

J. Denham Smith

THE POSSIBILITY OF WORSHIP

Worship, then, is required of every believer. As we face that responsibility, let us be encouraged that worship is possible for every believer. We have already thought about the detailed instructions given by God to govern the offering of His people. The opening chapters of Leviticus outline the rules for five different offerings – the burnt offering, the meat offering, the peace offering, the sin offering, and the trespass offering. Some of these offerings – the sin offering and the trespass offering – have to do with the putting away of sin. The others are the sweet savour offerings. In them, we have Christ, presented to God in all His perfection. These offerings represent the worship offered to God by His redeemed people.

It is noteworthy that the regulations for all the offerings stipulate a range of sacrifices that can be offered. So, for example, the burnt offering could consist of a bull, a male sheep or goat, or two turtledoves or pigeons (Lev. 1:3–17). Similarly, in the case of the sin offering, the acceptable sacrifices ranged all the way from a bull to two turtledoves and even, in the case of extreme poverty, to an offering of fine flour (Lev. 4–5). Two precious truths emerge from this. Firstly, God, in His grace, made provision for the putting away of the sins of all. The range of sacrifices that He would deign to accept meant that no-one was too poor to have their sin forgiven and to be made right with God. And this universally accessible provision beautifully foreshadows the work of Christ and the salvation that He would provide 'without money and without price' (Isa. 55:1). The diversity of the prescribed sacrifices illustrates another point. All were to offer according to their ability. As the fires of the altar consumed the sweet savour offerings, the wealthy man's bullock was not more precious to God than the two tiny turtledoves that were all a poor man could afford. God desired worship from every section and stratum of society, and graciously He made it possible for all to offer.

God accepts the humblest act of worship. More than that, He appreciates it. Nowhere is this more beautifully illustrated than in Mark 12, as the Lord Jesus 'sat over against the treasury, and beheld how the people cast money into the treasury' (v. 41). There, amid the flashy ostentation of the wealthy, and amid the clatter of their rich offerings, the Saviour saw a lonely widow, and heard the sound of two mites falling into the treasury. Her offering made very little contribution to the wealth of the temple, and was hardly worth a movement of the accountant's pen. But to the Lord, its value was inestimable, and His commendation of her recorded God's appreciation of a worshipper who gives the little all she has:

> Verily I say unto you, That this poor widow hath cast more in, than all they which have cast into the treasury: For all they did cast in of their abundance; but she of her want did cast in all that she had, even all her living (Mk 12:43–4).

This ought to encourage us greatly. It is easy to be intimidated by the fluency and fervour of the worship offered by older and more experienced brethren. As we listen to their praise, enriched and sweetened by a lifetime of communion with God, we are often acutely conscious of how inadequate our few poorly expressed thoughts seem. But God still desires our worship, and no appreciation of His Son is too small, or too ineloquent to rejoice His heart. He looks for bullocks from those with large capacity, but do not let us imagine that He will ever disregard or despise the smallest turtledove of the youngest believer.

THE PROGRESSION OF WORSHIP

The gradated requirements for sacrifice remind us, then, that worship is possible for all. But they also remind us that development in worship is possible. There is always potential for us to offer more than we have before, to have our capacity and capability enlarged beyond their existing constraints. The man who brought the pair of turtledoves knew that his offering was acceptable to and appreciated by God, but it would be strange if he did not look at the bullock offered by his wealthy neighbour and feel his heart swell with a spiritual ambition that one day he, too, would be in a position to offer an equally expensive offering to God.

We should feel something of the same spiritual ambition. In all aspects of our service for God, it is easy for us to settle for the status quo, and to lose the spirit that led Jabez famously to pray:

> Oh that Thou wouldest bless me indeed, and enlarge my coast, and that Thine hand might be with me, and that Thou wouldest keep me from evil, that it may not grieve me (1 Chron. 4:10).

Jabez may well have been a young man – certainly his prayer, while appropriate to be echoed by every saint, is especially fitting on the lips of a younger believer. A similar spirit was manifest in the old man, Caleb, as he claimed the promise of God, regardless of the formidable difficulties that came with the fulfilment of the promise:

> I am this day fourscore and five years old. As yet I am as strong this day as I was in the day that Moses sent me: as my strength was then, even so is my strength now, for war, both to go out, and to come in. Now therefore give me this mountain, whereof the LORD spake in that day; for thou heardest in that day how the Anakims were there, and that the cities were great and fenced: if so be the LORD will be with me, then I shall be able to drive them out, as the LORD said (Josh. 14:10–12).

The example of these two men of God ought to inspire and motivate us to determine that we will not, like

Moab, simply 'settle on our lees' (Jer. 48:11), but that we will continually seek to be more, to do more, to give more, and to worship more.

THE EXPENSE OF WORSHIP

But we should be conscious that this ambition will not be fulfilled without considerable expenditure on our part. Worship is costly. If we were inclined to doubt this, a glance back over the characters that we have noted in earlier chapters ought to convince us. Think of the woman in Matthew 26, who poured a year's salary over the Saviour's feet. Think of the widow, in Mark 12, who gave all she had. Or think of Abraham who was prepared to offer his son, 'his only Isaac' whom he loved (Gen. 22:2). Or, pre-eminently, think of God's Only-begotten Son, 'Who through the eternal Spirit offered himself without spot to God' (Heb. 9:14).

Faced with such examples as these, we cannot but conclude that worship is a costly exercise. We do not develop as worshippers automatically or unwittingly. Development in this most sacred of activities will demand conscious effort and application, and will require sacrifice on our part. We will not develop our capacity to worship by listening to the driving bass and the vacuous repetitions of contemporary Christian music. We will not be better equipped to offer the sacrifices of praise by spending time socialising with our friends, whether in person or through social networking. And, it needs hardly be said, our hearts and hands will not be filled with worship by the cultural products of a fallen world that 'lieth in the evil one' (1 Jn 5:19). And, while we may be helped to worship by the writings or words of believers whose appreciation of God is deeper than our own, these are not the only or the best guides to the development of our worship. For that we can only turn to the Word of God.

CHAPTER 10

WORSHIP DEMONSTRATED (I)

WORSHIP IN THE PSALMS

IF WE SEEK to develop as worshippers, there is one resource, above all others, to which we can turn. In the pages of our Bibles we learn what worship is. We learn Who it is that we worship, and why and how we are to worship Him. Romans 1 makes it clear that there is a close relationship between revelation and worship:

> Because that which may be known of God is manifest in them; for God hath shewed it unto them. For the invisible things of Him from the creation of the world are clearly seen, being understood by the things that are made, even His eternal power and Godhead; so that they are without excuse: Because that, when they knew God, they glorified Him not as God, neither were thankful; ... Who changed the truth of God into a lie, and worshipped and served the creature more than the Creator, Who is blessed for ever. Amen (Rom. 1:19–21, 25).

Had God not made Himself known in creation, mankind would have had neither the responsibility nor the possibility of worshipping God. It was because God had made something of His greatness and goodness known that man ought to have responded with worship and thanksgiving. Throughout the Bible we have examples of those who did respond with worship to God's creatorial revelation, and we can hardly contemplate the splendours of nature without being moved to worship the God Who designed the worlds and brought them into being with a word. Throughout Scripture, we find God worshipped as the Creator, and this aspect of His being is one of the chief themes of heavenly worship:

> And when those beasts give glory and honour and thanks to Him that sat on the throne, who liveth for ever and ever, The four and twenty elders fall down before Him that sat on the throne, and worship Him that liveth for ever and ever, and cast their crowns before the throne, saying, Thou art worthy, O Lord, to receive glory and honour and power: for Thou hast created all things, and for Thy pleasure they are and were created (Rev. 4:9–11).

But we have an even greater revelation of God than the immensities and intricacies of nature. In the Scriptures, God has given us a sufficient revelation of Himself. To know God is prerequisite to worshipping God, and it is in the pages of His holy Word that we come to know God. And as we grow in our knowledge of God, so too will we grow in our compulsion and our capacity to worship Him.

Scripture, then, teaches us Who we worship. But it also tells us why we worship. When we think of worship in the Old Testament, our thoughts inevitably turn to the book of Psalms. The Psalms are Israel's songbook, and it is hardly surprising that, among the many themes that they touch, they contain much worship. Psalms 95 to 100 are a particularly interesting study in this regard. They are especially concerned with worship, and form a distinct group within the Psalms. According to 'strong tradition supported by the LXX [the Septuagint, i.e. the Greek translation of Hebrew Scripture] titles to 95 – 97, these psalms were used at the dedication of the second temple.[*] Today, along with Psalm 29, Psalm 95 to 99 form the Kabbalat Shabbat, the Friday night prayers which introduce the Sabbath. With their repeated calls to worship and praise God, these Psalms are a striking and stirring expression of the greatness and worth of God. A detailed consideration of their content would require a volume to itself. We will briefly mention some important lessons that lie on the surface of these inspired songs of worship.

In Psalm 95, the Psalmist's focus is what God has done for His people.[†] In verse 1, He is the Redeemer: 'the Rock of our salvation'. In verse 6, we are called to worship the Creator: 'O come, let us worship and bow down: let us kneel before the LORD our maker'. Verse 7 presents Him as the protector, the Shepherd of His own: 'He is our God; and we are the people of His pasture, and the sheep of His hand'. It is good if our worship begins where this Psalm does. As we think of all that God has done on our behalf, of His power as Creator, of the price He paid for our redemption, and of His on-going preservation and protection of His own, our hearts too should be touched. It is instructive to notice the escalation of praise presented in the Psalm. It commences with singing (v. 1), progresses to

---

[*] Arthur G. Clarke, *Analytical Studies in the Psalms*, (Grand Rapids, MI: Kregel, 1979), 237

[†] Hebrews 4:7 indicates that this Psalm is one of the many written by King David.

thanksgiving (v. 2), and then reaches the heights of worship (v. 6). In some of what is written or said about worship, there is a tendency to contrast it with thanksgiving, and to disparage praise as being inferior to worship. As presented to us in this Psalm, however, they are intimately intertwined, and the man who begins with praise and thanksgiving does not have to move too far until he is bowed low in worship.

Psalm 95 focuses primarily on Israel. Both the terms of the praise and the warning that makes up the last section of the Psalm indicate that it is the nation that is especially in view. As we move to Psalm 96 we find that the scope of worship goes far beyond the boundaries of Israel. Now it is 'all the earth' (v. 1) and 'all people' (v. 3) who are invited to worship. And the focus here is not primarily upon what God has done, but upon the supremacy of His person. He is presented to us in this Psalm as the God Who is without peer:

> For the LORD is great, and greatly to be praised: He is to be feared above all gods. For all the gods of the nations are idols: but the LORD made the heavens (Ps. 96:4–5).

The Psalm expresses not so much an invitation to worship, as an imperative to worship. The threefold repetition of 'sing' in the first two verses, and of 'give unto the LORD' in verses 7 and 8 give 'a holy urgency ... almost [an] impatience' to David's call for worship.[*] And David's burning desire is that all the earth would 'give unto the LORD the glory due unto His name' (v. 8). This worship stands in stark contrast to the heathen adoration of 'the gods of the nations'. They were idols, and neither did nor could deserve the worship that was

---

[*] J.M. Flanigan, *What the Bible Teaches: Psalms*, (Kilmarnock: John Ritchie, 2001), 409–10.

offered to them. In worshipping God, we are only giving what is His due, for 'honour and majesty are before Him: strength and beauty are in His sanctuary' (v. 6).

The worship that David demands – and that God deserves – is commensurate with His greatness and His character: 'O worship the LORD in the beauty of holiness' (v. 9). This great injunction occurs on two other occasions in our Bibles, in 1 Chronicles 16:29, and Psalm 29:2. It reminds us that there are requirements for worship. The call to praise God sounded in this Psalm goes out to all the earth. It is directed to those who have been involved in the false worship of idol gods. But it is not a call simply to replace these gods with God as the object of worship. David has a far more radical transformation in view. False worship will do for false gods, a Holy God must be worshipped in the beauty of holiness. This is a solemn lesson for us all to learn, and if we feel the weight of this threefold injunction it must cause us to search our hearts and consciences, and to ensure that we are, in truth, worshipping God in the beauty of holiness.

Psalm 97 begins where Psalm 96 ended – with the LORD reigning. The focus of this Psalm is not on what God has done, but upon what He will do. It is millennial in its content, looking forward to the day when He will reign, and His righteousness will be seen. This is unmistakably a Psalm about the manifestation of the character of God. The keynote of that character is righteousness. 'Righteousness and judgment are the habitation of His throne' (v. 2), and as He reigns, that righteousness radiates outwards until it fills all creation. This righteousness is felt by his enemies: 'A fire goeth before Him, and burneth up His enemies round about' (v. 3). It is manifest, too, to a wondering world: 'The heavens declare His righteousness, and all the people see His glory' (v. 6). Before such incandescent righteousness, there is no alternative but to worship. Even the idol gods of the heathen must worship. Just as the image of Dagon fell on its face before the ark (1 Sam. 5), so every idol must fall in acknowledgement of the supremacy of Jehovah.

The theme of the holiness of God is taken up again in Psalm 99. Three times in the psalm the holiness of Jehovah is emphasised (vv. 3, 5, 9), leading Spurgeon to describe this as 'the holy, holy, holy psalm'.[*] Like Psalm 97, this Psalm begins with Jehovah reigning. In Psalm 97, the consequence of His reign was global rejoicing; in this psalm 'the people tremble' (v. 1) in reverential fear. 'Awesome' is a word that has been beggared of much of its proper significance, but in the fullest meaning of the word, God is presented in this psalm as awesome. He is to be worshipped, but not familiarly, to be praised, but not casually. Each of the three calls to worship is linked with the holiness of God:

> Let them praise Thy great and terrible name; for it is holy (v. 3).
>
> Exalt ye the LORD our God, and worship at his footstool; for He is holy (v. 5).
>
> Exalt the LORD our God, and worship at His holy hill; for the LORD our God is holy (v. 9).

There is nothing superficial about the worship that is called for in these verses. It is the antithesis of so much of what passes for worship in contemporary evangelicalism. And these verses are an acid test for our own worship. Do I approach God in reverential trembling? Do I come with an awareness of the holiness

---

[*] C.H. Spurgeon, *The Treasury of David*, (London: Marshall Brothers, n.d.), IV, 222

of His great and terrible name? Does my worship take its character from the God to Whom it is offered?

We worship God because of what He has done. But we worship Him too because of Who He is. And as we think of His character, we cannot but think of His righteousness and holiness. It was this Divine attribute of which the angels sang, when Isaiah saw 'the LORD sitting upon a throne, high and lifted up' (Isa. 6:1), and heard the refrain of the seraphim – 'Holy, holy, holy, is the LORD of hosts' (v. 3). But this is not the only attribute of God that should command our worship. Rather, every facet of His perfection should move us to adore Him. And, while David could look forward to a millennial manifestation of Divine righteousness, we rejoice in a far fuller revelation of God than Israel's sweet psalmist ever enjoyed. To us, 'in these last days' God has spoken 'in His Son, ... the brightness of His glory, and the express image of His person' (Heb. 1:1, 3). As we trace His footsteps through the pages of the inspired record, we see the character of God manifest in all its fulness –in His grace, His mercy, and His love – and in His perfect righteousness.

These psalms provide us with something of a template for our worship. They help us to understand why we worship and they exemplify for us the contemplations that will cause us to worship. As we think of what God has done, and meditate on His goodness, our thankfulness for the individual blessings that we have received will swell and soar into worship. From there, it is only a small step to the contemplation of the greatness of God. He is unique in His being, solitary in His might, and His glory He will not give to another (Isa. 42:8). As we dwell upon His supremacy, our hearts echo the question posed in song by Moses and the children of Israel:

> Who is like unto Thee, O LORD, among the gods? Who is like Thee, glorious in holiness, fearful in praises, doing wonders? (Exod. 15:11).

And, as these words demonstrate, our meditation upon the greatness of God will lead us to contemplate His glories, the many and marvellous attributes that all contribute to His glory.

These psalms remind us that we develop our worship by considering God. As we get to know more of God, through the reading and study of, and meditation upon His Word, so we will find worship deepen and develop. It is important to notice that, while these psalms do provide a template for worship, they do not embody a rigid taxonomy. As we have seen, worship begets worship. Nor should we be too concerned to make distinctions about the value of different kinds of worship. There is progression in these psalms, but not hierarchy. There is little as paralysing to our worship as the nagging concern that we are, somehow, not offering the best kind of worship. We have seen that God expects precision in worship; He does not demand pedantry. If we fill our minds with God and His word, we will and we must worship, and that worship will be both acceptable and valuable to Him.

Chapter 11

Worship Demonstrated (II)

Worship in New Testament Song

IN THE PRECEDING CHAPTERS of this book we have learned something about the importance that our worship has for God, and the consequent importance that it must have for us. We have seen that worship is the responsibility of every believer, and that each believer must, therefore, be exercised about developing his or her ability to offer to God the worship that He seeks. We have noted the importance of God's Word in developing our ability to worship. As we have considered the pictures and the psalms of Old Testament Scripture, we have considered the principles that they embody, and the pattern that they provide for worship. In this chapter, we turn our attention to the New Testament, to discover whether it provides us with any exemplars of worship for the dispensation of grace. We find these exemplars especially in the songs and the prayers recorded for us throughout the pages of the New Testament.

The book of Psalms is the hymnbook of Israel. In it we find songs of rejoicing and celebration. We find deeply moving expressions of sorrow, of loss, of failure and repentance. And, as we have seen in the previous chapter, we also find great and glorious hymns of worship and of praise. Notwithstanding the cultural, chronological, and dispensational distance that separates us from the original singers of these songs, they offer us still a valuable prototype for our worship.

There is no New Testament equivalent to the Psalms. No book of Scripture provides us with access to the hymnal of the early Church. The epistles do, however, demonstrate that the singing of hymns was part of the practice of first-century believers, both individually and collectively. So, for example, James encouraged the believers to whom he wrote to bring every circumstance of life before God: 'Is any among you afflicted? let him pray. Is any merry? let him sing psalms' (Jas. 5:13). Writing to the Colossians and the Ephesians, the Apostle Paul emphasised that hymns should have a communal role, as well as an individual:

> Let the word of Christ dwell in you richly in all wisdom; teaching and admonishing one another in psalms and hymns and spiritual songs, singing with grace in your hearts to the Lord (Col. 3:16).

> And be not drunk with wine, wherein is excess; but be filled with the Spirit; Speaking to yourselves in psalms and hymns and spiritual songs, singing and making melody in your heart to the Lord (Eph. 5:19).

Similarly, his words to the believers at Corinth confirm that, for these first-century believers, singing psalms (a term which probably encompasses what we would call hymns, in addition to the psalms of Scripture) was a normal part of assembly gatherings and, especially, the breaking of bread:

How is it then, brethren? when ye come together, every one of you hath a psalm, hath a doctrine, hath a tongue, hath a revelation, hath an interpretation. Let all things be done unto edifying (1 Cor. 14:26).

We would give a good deal to have access to the Corinthians' – or the Apostle's – hymnbook, to know the words they sang as they gathered together to 'show forth the Lord's death' (1 Cor. 11:26). In the providence of God, however, this has not been preserved. Nonetheless, the epistles of the New Testament may preserve for us traces of the hymns sung by believers in the first century. There are a number of portions in Paul's writings whose form and vocabulary differ from their immediate context in a way that has lead New Testament scholars to argue that they are portions of pre-existing hymns, incorporated by the apostle, under Divine inspiration, and becoming part of God's Word. Different scholars apply different criteria, and produce longer or shorter lists, but there is general – though not universal – agreement that Philippians 2:6-11; Colossians 1:15-20; and 1 Timothy 3:16 are examples of these interpolated hymns.

It is beyond the scope or intention of this book to look at the arguments that can be made for and against viewing these passages of Scripture as portions of hymns. Whichever view we take does nothing to diminish the status or significance, to undermine the inspiration of these verses, or the fundamental doctrine that they contain. If, however, we do take it that these verses were originally sung as hymns, they teach us some valuable lessons about the nature and purpose of hymnody.

The most striking thing about these verses is their doctrinal content. Each of these passages is a theological bolus. With economy of expression, they compress a profound wealth of theological truth into a very small span. A few minutes, at most, would suffice to read them, but adequately to understand – still less to expound – the truth that they contain is a life's work. The believers of the first century, it would seem, were not content to spend their time singing the same platitudes over and over again. Nor did they find it helpful to spend their time singing songs that were designed merely to express emotion, and to stimulate and evoke still further emotion. As they sang, they were giving expression to fundamental and fathomless doctrines concerning the person of the Lord Jesus Christ.

It is not difficult to understand why this was so. Levels of literacy were far lower in the first century than they are in most parts of world today, and many if not most believers would have been unable to read Scripture for themselves. Instead, they had to rely on the public reading of the Word of God. This circumstance accounts for Paul's instruction to Timothy to 'give attendance to reading' (1 Tim. 4:13). When confronted with questionable doctrine, these early believers did not always have the option of taking down their Bibles, and determining from its pages the truth of what they had been taught. In this context, it was particularly useful to have Scriptural doctrine in a form that could be memorised easily, and that would be reinforced by constant singing.

And even in these early days, believers had a good deal of false teaching to contend with. The precious truths of the Deity and humanity of the Lord Jesus Christ were coming under intense and sustained attack from judaising and gnostic teachings. This made it all the more necessary for believers to be continuously reminded of the Scriptural truth regarding the person and work of the Lord Jesus Christ. It is not a coincidence that it is in the epistle to the Colossians – which was written particularly to counter Christological error, that the Apostle Paul insists on the value of hymns to teach and admonish God's people:

> teaching and admonishing one another in psalms and hymns and spiritual songs, singing with grace in your hearts to the Lord (Col. 3:16)

These hymns, with their concentrated Christological content, were well suited to strengthen and preserve the believers in a world filled with false doctrine.

Our world is a very different place from that of the first century. We have ready access to the completed canon of Scripture and, for the most part, are able to read God's Word for ourselves. But truth is still under attack, and hymns still have a vital role to play in encapsulating, expressing, and inculcating scriptural doctrine. We have a solid heritage of soundly doctrinal hymns that express our worship even as they edify our hearts. These hymns are not great because of the virtuosity of their composition – many, if not most of them, are musically very simple. Nor do they rely for their impact on the skill with which they are performed, or the grandeur of their orchestration. They are not great because they are old, or because they were enjoyed by an earlier generation – though many of them are and were. Like the hymns that rose so readily to the Apostle's mind, they are great because they are doctrinal – because they embody the truths of God's Word and express them so as to make them memorable.

Not all hymns meet this standard, and we are, at times, surprisingly willing to give expression in song to teaching that would raise our eyebrows, and perhaps our hackles, if we heard it propounded from platform or pulpit. We can at times allow a felicitous turn of phrase or an appealing melody to sugar teaching that is frankly unscriptural. This willingness to tolerate in poetry what we would reject in prose can only be accounted for on the basis of an implicit assumption that the content of our hymns is not really important. Nothing could be further from the truth. Hymns have an ability to work their way under our skins and in to our hearts and souls that is only seldom equalled by preaching or teaching. As we sing them week-by-week, they inevitably and inexorably form our thinking and shape our understanding.

This being so, it is a matter of immense importance to ensure that the content of the hymns we sing – at all times, but perhaps especially when we sing of Christ – is in accord with the teaching of Scripture. This is not to say that we should engage in nit-picking or pedantry just for the sake of it. But we should make sure that the statements and sentiments that we sing contain and confirm scriptural doctrine, rather than contradicting or undermining it.

This imperative is especially pressing in the case of contemporary Christian music. It is not the case that new hymns are inevitably bad – any more than it is true that old hymns are guaranteed to be good. After all, we must remember that the hymns that Paul quoted cannot have been much more than twenty years old. Nonetheless, it would be foolish to disregard the fact that the passage of time does act as a filter, straining out the ephemeral or merely trendy, and providing a more accurate perspective on the enduring value of a particular hymn.

There are undoubtedly many modern compositions that are firmly based on Scripture, that exalt Christ, and edify the saints. We should welcome these to our hearts and our hymnbooks. But it is undeniable that much contemporary Christian music is doctrinally vacuous. It is often clear that it has been composed with the priority of providing an electrifying and exciting performance. Shorn of their belting bass lines and thundering choruses, these songs shrink to a selection of sentimental slogans that do little to admonish, instruct, or edify.

Scripture is full of song. The 'morning stars sang together' (Job 38:7) as Creation bloomed before their wondering gaze. Israel sang on the banks of the Red Sea, praising God for His power and for the deliverance He had brought. Deborah, too, sang of deliverance, of the overthrow of the oppressor, and of the liberation of God's people (Judg. 5). The disciples sang and, moving towards the cross, the Lord sang with them (Mt. 26:30). Heaven will reverberate with songs old and new, for mingled with the strains of the new song will be 'Moses the servant of God, and the song of the Lamb' (Rev. 15:3). We will sing in Heaven (Rev. 4–5), and it would be strange if we did not desire to anticipate that occupation by adding our strains to the songs of the saints. We should sing; we must sing. But as we do, let us remember that our psalms as well as our prayers must be offered 'in spirit and in truth'. Enriched, as we are, by a noble heritage of great hymns, we have no need to settle for the sentimental, saccharine, or second-rate.

Worship and Music

Let us imagine for a moment that we are sitting, on a Lord's Day morning, waiting for the Breaking of Bread to commence. The hall is silent – as it should be – with only the occasional crackle of a Bible page to disturb the stillness. But then the silence is broken. Outside, in the foyer, we hear the sound of a man's voice. It's unfamiliar, but unremarkable, and beyond idly wondering who is visiting we are unmoved. But then we hear another sound – the lowing of a bullock. It is unexpected and shocking, but entirely unmistakable, and a ripple of curiosity runs around the company as every ear is strained to hear what is happening in the vestibule.

Outside the scene is startling. The brethren who are manning the doors are confronting a pleasant, well-dressed man, who would be in no way alarming, were he not holding the halter of a large and indignant bullock. Raising his voice to be heard above the commotion, he explains that he has come to worship, and that this bullock is his peace offering, and enquires where he ought to take it, in order for it to be butchered. Aghast, the brethren gather themselves together sufficiently to explain that animal sacrifices were a feature of Old Testament worship, and they have no place in the dispensation of grace. The man responds that he realises that there is no direct New Testament mandate for the continued use of animal sacrifices, but that he finds them enormously moving, and tremendously helpful in assisting his worship.

Now this is clearly nothing more than a flight of fancy. But can you imagine how we would respond in the – admittedly highly unlikely – event that something like this happened? Depending on how phlegmatic the brethren involved were, their response would range from politely but firmly demanding that the animal be removed to calling the police. News of the incident would spread like wildfire, and it would inspire much conversation, headshaking, and tongue-clicking. We would be utterly taken aback, and rather appalled that we had been witnesses to such a thoroughgoing misunderstanding of the nature of worship in a New Testament setting.

Such an event seems unthinkable, but something almost exactly similar happens regularly in many places, and never excites comment, still less alarm. Elements of Old Testament worship are inappropriately incorporated into communal worship, without any scriptural mandate, simply on the basis that people find them helpful, because they make them feel like worshipping. No one wants to revive animal sacrifices – which would after all be expensive and terribly messy – but there is no shortage of those who would like to adopt the Old Testament practice of worshipping with music.

As we have seen, the New Testament provides us with a clear and unambiguous mandate for Christian song, and with examples of the sort of doctrinally-saturated, spiritually-stimulating songs that were part of the worship of first-century believers. By contrast, neither the Acts of the Apostles not the epistles record any precedent, practice, or precept that would validate the use of musical instruments in the worship of God.

This would come as a surprise to anyone who knew Christianity only through the lens of contemporary Christendom. For many believers, the role of music as an element of worship is something that is taken for granted. The nature of the music may vary: for some the sonorous blare of the organ is the most appropriate accompaniment; others prefer the more upbeat and informal rhythm of the guitar; while for some, worship would be incomplete without the cacophonous co-mingling of a full rock band. But, whatever the style, the appropriateness – even the necessity – of musical accompaniment is widely taken for granted.

This disconnection between the scriptural pattern and contemporary practice is striking. In an effort to bridge the gap, supporters of musical worship will often appeal to Old Testament Scripture. And it is clear that music did play a role in the service of the Temple. As David made arrangements for the ark to come up to Jerusalem, he appointed 'spake to the chief of the Levites to appoint their brethren to be the singers with instruments of musick, psalteries and harps and cymbals, sounding, by lifting up the voice with joy' (1 Chron. 15:16). Later, music played an important role in the Temple worship, and its restoration is specifically mentioned in the revival under Hezekiah:

> And he set the Levites in the house of the LORD with cymbals, with psalteries, and with harps, according to the commandment of David, and of Gad the king's seer, and Nathan the prophet: for so was the commandment of the LORD by His prophets. And the Levites stood with the instruments of David, and the priests with the trumpets (2 Chron. 29:25–26).

It must have been a remarkable experience to hear the Temple courts echo to the sweet strains of these expert musicians. And if their artistry and skill contributed to the worship of God in that day, surely we are justified in imitating it, even in the absence of an explicit New Testament mandate. After all, if it pleased God then, it must surely please Him now.

This is a specious argument, but its flaws must be recognised. In the Old Testament, this music was an integral part of the Temple service. It was the responsibility of selected Levites, who had their own particular instruments, and their own stations in the House of God. Their music was as closely linked with the Temple as the ministry of the priests, the animal sacrifices offered on the brazen altar, the showbread, and the incense arising from the golden altar.

Each of these elements was part of the larger system of worship. If we use the fact that music was part of Old Testament worship to warrant its continued use in the Church Age, we must be prepared to allow for the continuation of all the other elements of Old Testament worship. We cannot logically exclude any other part of the system, not an officiating priesthood, or clouds of incense, or animal sacrifices.

We are not, of course, very likely to attempt the wholesale revival of the Levitical system. If nothing else, such an effort would present formidable practical and logistical considerations, and the full restoration of the Levitical service is impossible, and will remain so until the Temple has been rebuilt. But there are some elements of the system that are so easy to revive or retain, that fit so easily into our gatherings, and that seem so useful in helping us to feel worshipful. Would it really be so problematic to use those elements in this dispensation?

The scriptural answer to this question is yes. In chapter 3 we have already considered the Saviour's description of the sort of worship that would mark the dispensation of grace. The shadowy, insubstantial worship of Judaism would come to an end, and true worshippers would worship the Father 'in spirit and in truth' (Jn 4:24). This true worship would leave behind all the geographical and physical features of worship under the Law, and would enter into the spiritual reality foreshadowed by the sights, the sounds, and the smells of Old Testament worship.

This worship would be 'in spirit'. By contrast, music belongs to the realm of the physical. C.H. Spurgeon, with his characteristically telling turn of phrase, said 'We might as well pray by machinery as praise by it', and his words neatly highlight the contrast between the spiritual and the physical and mechanical.* Furthermore, music operates in the emotional, rather than the spiritual, realm. There are few things that have the capacity to excite and engage our emotions that music does. Music can certainly make us feel like worshipping, but it does so only at the level of our emotions, and is likely to affect an unbeliever in just the same way as a believer. Its effects may be keenly felt, but they are fleeting and ephemeral.

Music also has the tendency to misdirect our attention. To be able to play a musical instrument well is a skill that we admire and appreciate. And in most settings there could be no difficulty with our acknowledging the ability and dedication that lie behind a virtuosic performance. However, such virtuosity, such human ability are a distraction from the true focus of our worship. That this is more than just a theoretical danger is eloquently confirmed by the CD racks of Christian bookstores, where the focus of liner photos, posters, and review comments is on the artists and their talent. We do well to bear in mind the truth that Paul impressed upon the pagan worshippers of Athens: God is not 'worshipped with men's hands' (Acts 17:25). The writer to the Hebrews exhorts us to offer to God 'the fruit of our lips', but makes no mention of the 'fruit of our fingers' (Heb. 13:15).

Earlier in this chapter, I stated that 'neither the Acts of the Apostles not the epistles record any precedent, practice, or precept that would validate the use of

---

* C.H. Spurgeon, *The Treasury of David*, II, 272

musical instruments in the worship of God.' That statement is true – with one exception. In Ephesians 5, the Apostle Paul outlines the nature of the Spirit-filled life:

> ...be filled with the Spirit; speaking to yourselves in psalms and hymns and spiritual songs, singing and making melody in your heart to the Lord (Eph. 5:18–19).

There is one musical instrument whose use is approved by the New Testament as part of the spiritual Christian's worship. This instrument is not found amongst the strings, the woodwind, or percussion sections of any orchestra. It produces neither tone nor timbre audible to human ears, but God delights to hear the melody of a well-tuned heart adding its inimitable harmony to the praise of the believers. On this instrument, we should all seek to become virtuosi, practising and rehearsing until no false note is sounded, no inharmonious resonance expressed. As we gather to worship we should leave our instruments – and our animals – at the door. But as we come, may we have melodious hearts as we sing the praises of our God.

Come, Thou Fount of every blessing,
Tune my heart to sing Thy grace;
Streams of mercy, never ceasing,
Call for songs of loudest praise.
Teach me some melodious sonnet,
Sung by flaming tongues above.
Praise the mount, I'm fixed upon it,
Mount of Thy redeeming love.
—Robert Robinson

NOTE – THE VERB *PSALLŌ* AND ITS IMPLICATIONS

Advocates of instrumental music have sometimes sought support for their position in the etymology of the Greek word *psallō* which is translated as 'sing' in Romans 15:9 and 1 Corinthians 14:15 (twice), as 'making melody' in Ephesians 5:19, and as 'sing psalms' in James 5:13. They point out that the word has, at its root, the idea of rubbing or touching. Over time, it developed the meaning of plucking or striking the strings of a musical instrument, and then, to sing. This derivation has led some to suggest that *psallō* has inherent in it the meaning of singing to accompaniment. This is a weak case for a number of reasons:

1. While the etymology of *psallō* may be linked to musical instruments, lexical experts are clear that, by the time the New Testament was written, the word no longer had any necessary link to musical accompaniment, but rather that 'sing' had become its main sense. (See, *inter alia*, William D. Mounce (ed.), *Mounce's Complete Expository Dictionary of Old and New Testament Words*, (Grand Rapids, MI: Zondervan, 2006), 659; Frederick William Danker, *A Greek-English Lexicon of the New Testament and other Early Christian Literature*, (Chicago, IL: University of Chicago Press, 2000), 1096; and Joseph Henry Thayer, *Greek-English Lexicon of the New Testament* (Grand Rapids, MI: Zondervan, 1962), 675. An extensive discussion of the meaning of *psallō* may be found in M.C. Kurfees, *Instrumental Music in the Worship or the Greek Verb Psallo Philologically and Historically Examined* (Nashville, TN: Gospel Advocate, 1999). It is worth stressing that the meaning of words

does change over time, and many English words now mean something quite different from what their etymological roots might suggest.

2. Historical evidence is clear that music was not introduced into communal Christian worship until the fifth century. If it were indeed the case that *psallō* clearly implies musical accompaniment, and that early believers had understood it in this way, we would have to explain a protracted, universal, and uncompromising disobedience to the Word of God. We do not depend on the Church Fathers for our guidance, but it is relevant to note their unanimous disapproval of instrumental music.

3. Even if we allow the possibility that *psallō* may imply musical accompaniment, its usage in the New Testament does not give us a mandate for the use of musical instruments in corporate worship. As mentioned above, the word occurs five times in the New Testament. In Romans 15:9, Paul follows the LXX in quoting 2 Samuel 22:50 or Psalm 18:49. The words quoted are David's, and the context has nothing to do with corporate worship. The same is true of James 5:13 – 'Is any among you afflicted? let him pray. Is any merry? let him sing psalms.' – which is clearly dealing with the private devotional life of the individual believer. We have dealt with Ephesians 5:19 above, and seen that the instrument in view here is not a mechanical contrivance of man's design, but the heart of the believer. That leaves us with 1 Corinthians 14:15: 'I will pray with the spirit, and I will pray with the understanding also: I will sing with the spirit, and I will sing with the understanding also'. The context here is Paul's treatment of tongues, and the necessity that they

be interpreted in order that the church might be edified. It is difficult to see how a focus on instrumental music fits this context – clearly Paul's focus is squarely on the singing as communication, that is, on the words that are sung. Not to put too fine a point on it, the verse is a rather forlorn hope as a justification for including musical instruments as part of our worship.

CHAPTER 12

WORSHIP DEMONSTRATED (III)

WORSHIP IN NEW TESTAMENT PRAYER

THERE IS MUCH that we can learn from the songs of Scripture, and a careful consideration of them will do much to encourage and elevate our worship. Similarly, the prayers of the New Testament and, especially, the doxologies of the New Testament epistles are a valuable study for any believer who wishes to develop his or her capacity to worship God.

The word doxology comes from two Greek words – *doxa*, meaning glory or praise; and *logos*, meaning word. They are 'short, spontaneous ascriptions of praise to God which frequently appear as concluding formulae to prayers, hymnic expressions, and sections of Paul's letters.'[*] We can helpfully see them as moments in the epistles when the focus moves from the horizontal to the vertical, as the writer ceases to address his readers in order to address God, to express the overflowing of his heart in spontaneous worship of God.

---

[*] Gerald F. Hawthorne, Ralph P. Martin and Daniel G. Reid, *Dictionary of Paul and His Letters* (Downers Grove, IL: InterVarsity Press, 1993), 'Doxology', *sv*.

Different readers of Scripture will apply different criteria for determining what exactly constitutes a doxology and will, consequently, produce lists that differ slightly. There are perhaps sixteen or seventeen doxologies on which there is general agreement.[*] Each of these contains a wealth of truth, and any sort of adequate survey of the doxologies would be a fairly hefty volume in its own right. Within the constraints of this chapter, we will focus on the doxologies recorded in the epistles and, in the available space, we can do little more than outline the importance of these portions of Scripture. For the purposes of this chapter, there are two aspects of these doxologies that are of particular interest – their content and their catalysts.

Even a cursory survey of the contents of the doxologies found in the New Testament epistles is sufficient to reveal how much they have in common. Each of the doxologies follows the same basic pattern. Firstly the object of worship is mentioned, then praise and glory are ascribed, and finally, the doxology usually closes with an eternity phrase – 'for ever and ever' and a concluding 'amen'. Each doxology, then, addresses a person, ascribes praise, and anticipates a period.

In keeping with what we have already seen of the pattern of biblical worship, the worship of the doxologies is ascribed only to Deity. Some of the doxologies are addressed to God the Father (see, for example, Rom. 16:27). Others are addressed to the Lord Jesus Christ (e.g. Rom. 9:5, 2 Pet. 3:18). A third category

---

[*] Rom 11:36; 16:27; Gal. 1:5; Eph. 3:21; Phil. 4:20; 1 Tim. 1:17; 1 Tim. 6:16; 2 Tim. 4:18; Heb. 13:21; 1 Pet. 4:11; 5:11; 2 Pet. 3:18; Jude 25; Rev. 1:5–6; 5:13; 7:12. See Brooke Foss Westcott, *The Epistle To The Hebrews: The Greek Text with Notes and Essays*, (London: Macmillan, 1903), 464–465. Westcott does not include Rom. 1:25 and 9:5, which do differ slightly in form from the other doxologies mentioned, but which will be included in our discussion here.

are addressed to the God, without distinguishing between the persons of the Godhead (e.g. 1 Tim 1:17). These doxologies are one of the striking proofs of the Deity of the Lord Jesus Christ – there is no distinction in the praise offered to the Father and the Son.

In their doxologies, the writers of inspired Scripture, ascribe praise to God. Glory speaks of worth made manifest, and our words can add nothing to the infinite and inherent glory of the Godhead. The same is true of the other terms that are used – honour, majesty, power, and dominion all belong absolutely and essentially to God. The purpose of these doxologies is not to add anything to Who and What God is. But the longing of the apostles' hearts is that the glory of God should be manifest and acknowledged in every corner and cranny of His creation. 'He must increase, but I must decrease' (Jn 3:30) is the prayer of every true worshipper, and as the writers of Scripture break out into doxology, their desire is for God to be glorified everywhere and for ever.

Many of the doxologies express a longing for the present glorification and magnification of the Father and the Son, but all anticipate an eternal period. Sometimes they speak of glory 'for ever' (literally, to the ages). At other times a strengthened form is used – 'for ever and ever', 'to the ages of the ages', the strongest term used in Greek to speak of eternity. 2 Peter 3:18 ascribes glory to the Lord Jesus Christ 'both now and to the day of eternity' (*Darby*). The point should not be missed. Worship has eternity for its timeframe. It is not occupied with the temporary or the passing. It is eternal in its aspiration, and eternal in its implications. It requires us, and allows us, to rise above the fleeting concerns and aspirations of this world. We desire, in the words of Lucy Meyer, to 'live with eternity's values in view'. And there is, perhaps, nothing that will so help adjust our sight and so alter our values to those of eternity as worshipping our God.

The content of the doxologies has much to teach us. There are also valuable lessons to be learned in the contexts and catalysts of the doxologies – in the considerations that motivate and produce their praise. It should come as no surprise to us that worship is the fruit of occupation with God. Each of these doxologies is inspired and occasioned by the writer's contemplation of the Godhead. It is worth stressing again that the catalysts of worship are external and objective, not internal and subjective. These words of praise bubble forth from a heart that is 'inditing a good matter' (Ps. 45:1), that has been warmed and moved by the contemplation of God and His Son. It is striking, however, that not one of these doxologies makes any allusion to the emotions or the feelings of the writer. The focus is always on God the Father, or the Lord Jesus Christ.

We should note how many of these doxologies follow some of the most detailed and fundamental doctrinal discussions of the New Testament. And this connection is not just an accident of sequence. Whether it be the forensic treatise of Romans, the Christological and typological discussions of the epistle to the Hebrews, or the ecclesiological expositions of Ephesians, there is a close and organic relationship between doctrine and worship. Thus, the worship of the doxologies is doubly worship 'in truth'. It expresses truth, but it also originates in truth.

Attempting too rigorously to categorise the catalysts of the doxologies would be an artificial and arid business. However, it is helpful to notice that these words of glory result from the writers' contemplation of Divine persons, Divine purpose, and Divine power.

The Doxologies and Divine Power

A number of the doxologies of the New Testament are motivated by the consideration of the magnitude of Divine power:

> Now unto Him that is able to do exceeding abundantly above all that we ask or think, according to the power that worketh in us, unto Him be glory in the church by Christ Jesus throughout all ages, world without end. Amen (Eph. 3:20–21).

> But my God shall supply all your need according to His riches in glory by Christ Jesus. Now unto God and our Father be glory for ever and ever. Amen (Phil. 4:19–20).

> And the Lord shall deliver me from every evil work, and will preserve me unto His heavenly kingdom: to Whom be glory for ever and ever. Amen (2 Tim. 4:18).

> Now the God of peace, that brought again from the dead our Lord Jesus, that great Shepherd of the sheep, through the blood of the everlasting covenant, make you perfect in every good work to do His will, working in you that which is wellpleasing in His sight, through Jesus Christ; to whom be glory for ever and ever. Amen (Heb. 13:20–21)

> But the God of all grace, who hath called us unto His eternal glory by Christ Jesus, after that ye have suffered a while, make you perfect, stablish, strengthen, settle you. To Him be glory and dominion for ever and ever. Amen (1 Pet. 5:10–11).

> Now unto Him that is able to keep you from falling, and to present you faultless before the presence of His glory with exceeding joy, to the only wise God our Saviour, be glory and majesty, dominion and power, both now and ever. Amen (Jude 24–25).

These expressions of worship spring directly from the writers' appreciation of the power of God. As they consider His super-abundant ability to meet every need of His people, they are moved to go beyond prayer, to praise and worship God.

These doxologies remind us that worship is an intensely practical business. If it is true that 'the people that do know their God shall be strong, and do exploits' (Dan. 11:32), and if it is indeed the case that worship is the inevitable result of a deepening knowledge of God, then it follows that there is a close relationship between our worship and our faith. Some times, we treat worship as a perfunctory prelude to our prayer, almost as though we hoped that we would flatter God into answering, but here the order is reversed. The realisation that God has the power to answer the prayer that is being expressed leads these men to adore God, as their prayer leads to worship.

In these doxologies, Paul, Peter, and Jude all attest God's ability. Repeatedly, they stress that He is able: able to keep, to establish, and to do above all that we ask or think. They rejoice, too, in God's abundance, in the bounty of Divine resources. God is able beyond what we ask or think – not just above our asking, or abundantly above our asking, but 'exceedingly abundantly above'. The scale of Divine power transcends expression, and the Apostle piles up superlatives to convey the vast extent of the power of God. God supplies in accordance with His 'glorious riches in Christ Jesus' (Phil. 4:19, ISV). He will guard the apostle not just from some or from most of the onslaughts of evil, but from every evil work. And we need never, even for a moment, doubt His power, for it is the self-same power that 'brought again from the dead our Lord Jesus'.

God's ability is not just abundant in its power, it is enduring in its duration. Paul is assured that the Lord is able to bring him safely to His heavenly kingdom. Peter is equally confident that the God Who 'called us unto His eternal glory by Christ Jesus' will keep us safely until we reach that resplendent destination. Jude affirms that God is able to preserve, purify, and present His own, flawless, and with great joy. And, lest this threefold testimony had left the scintilla of a doubt, the writer of the Hebrews praises the God Who is able to make the believer 'perfect in every good work.'

Our God is able, abundantly, eternally, omnipotently able. In each of these doxologies, this truth comes home with force to the heart of the writer, and wrings from their lips and pens words of worship. May we grasp His greatness as they did, and join with them to adore our able, our almighty, our awe-inspiring God.

The Doxologies and Divine Purpose

Worship results from an appreciation of the scale of Divine power. At other times, the doxologies are motivated by the sublime grandeur of the Divine purpose. On three occasions in Paul's writings (Rom. 11:33–36; 16:25–27; Gal. 1:35) his awe at the scale and sweep of God's great redemptive plan causes him to break into worship. Romans 11:33–36 is perhaps the best-known of the doxologies:

> O the depth of the riches both of the wisdom and knowledge of God! How unsearchable are His judgments, and His ways past finding out! For who hath known the mind of the Lord? or who hath been His counsellor? Or who hath first given to Him, and it shall be recompensed unto him again? For of Him, and through Him, and to Him, are all things: to Whom be glory for ever. Amen.

In the first eleven chapters of the epistle to the Romans, the apostle has moved from the depths of gloom as, in the opening chapters, he demonstrates the guilt of all humanity, to the heights of justification, liberation, and glorification, in chapters five to eight. He has traced the unfolding of God's great dispensational plan, and His abiding faithfulness to, and glorious purpose for the nation of Israel. Now, as he arrives at the pivot of this great epistle, he looks back over the ground that he has traversed. As he sees the infinite and unsearchable wisdom of God displayed in the temporal outworking of His eternal purpose, he responds with a great prayer of worship and adoration to the God from Whom, through Whom, and to Whom are all things.

The contemplation of the greatness of Divine wisdom motivates Paul's lip worship in this great doxology. It also motivates the life worship for which he calls in the following verses:

> I beseech you therefore, brethren, by the mercies of God, that ye present your bodies a living sacrifice, holy, acceptable unto God, which is your reasonable service. And be not conformed to this world: but be ye transformed by the renewing of your mind, that ye may prove what is that good, and acceptable, and perfect, will of God (Rom. 12:1–2).

It is important to grasp that the 'therefore' of verse one refers us back to the words of Paul's doxology, and thus to all of the first eleven chapters of the epistle. It is surely a mistake to limit the force of the 'therefore' to the first five chapters of the epistle. To be sure, God's mighty Gospel design should cause us to worship. But so too should the wisdom displayed in His ordering of the dispensations; the 'goodness and severity' (Rom. 11:22) demonstrated in the temporary setting aside of Israel and the blessing of the Gentiles; and the great purpose of blessing that underlies it all:

> For if the casting away of them be the reconciling of the world, what shall the receiving of them be, but life from the dead? (Rom. 11:15)

If we can think of these mighty subjects without bowing our hearts and knees to imitate the Apostle in his worship, there is something seriously amiss. Let us enlarge our minds to appreciate the scale of God's great purpose, its sublime wisdom, and its matchless grace. And let us worship and wonder as we grasp afresh the greatness of our God.

And as we grasp this, let us be sure that we respond as we ought – with an unstinting and unreserved 'living sacrifice'. True worship cannot be merely from the lips out – it must radiate from the heart. And it must radiate not just to our mouths, but to all our members, to every extremity of our being, and be manifest not just in what we say, but in what we do.

While Isaac Watts probably had Galatians 6:14 in mind when he wrote 'When I survey the wondrous cross', the imagery and implications of these verses were captured with tremendous beauty in the words of his famous hymn. One of the striking features of this hymn is its use of the word 'survey'. When Watts wrote the hymn, this word still possessed its scientific meaning. A survey was a prolonged, in-depth, comprehensive study, often of land or property. The word did not speak of a passing glance or a brief overview, but of prolonged and detailed scrutiny. As we work our way through the riches of the Roman epistle, we 'survey the wondrous cross'. May God grant that the experience would cause us to sing with meaning and truth:

> *When I survey the wondrous cross*
> *On which the Prince of glory died,*
> *My richest gain I count but loss,*
> *And pour contempt on all my pride.*
>
> *Were the whole realm of nature mine,*
> *That were an offering far too small.*
> *Love so amazing, so divine,*
> *demands my soul, my life, my all.*

The doxology of Romans 11 is occasioned by the scale of Divine intelligence, by the inscrutability and unknowablity of God, by the realisation that His thoughts far transcend the apprehension of even the finest human mind. At the end of the epistle, Paul worships again, and this time his worship is prompted and produced by the fact that this unsearchable and unfathomable God has caused His purpose – and His person – to be known:

> Now to Him that is of power to stablish you according to my gospel, and the preaching of Jesus Christ, according to the revelation of the mystery, which was kept secret since the world began, but now is made manifest, and by the scriptures of the prophets, according to the commandment of the everlasting God, made known to all nations for the

obedience of faith: to God only wise, be glory through Jesus Christ for ever. Amen (Rom. 16:25-27).

From the opening chapters of the epistle, Paul has spoken of a God Who has made Himself known. Whether by Creation, or by conscience, or, supremely, by the gospel, He has revealed Himself to mankind. Without these revelations, man could never have known God, never conceived of His goodness or His power, never have grasped anything of His wisdom. But God has spoken, has opened His purpose to mankind, and has made Himself known. And God's revelation of His person and purpose has not been sparing or restricted. He has not confined it to a chosen nation or a restricted class of initiates, but has published it to all nations. The words of Paul's doxology take us to the ascension of the Lord Jesus, and call to mind His commission to the disciples: 'ye shall be witnesses unto me both in Jerusalem, and in all Judaea, and in Samaria, and unto the uttermost part of the earth' (Acts 1:8). The doxology takes us back to Pentecost when, for the first time, God spoke in the language of the Gentiles. The Spirit-filled apostles spoke forth the wonderful works of God (Acts 2:11) in the language of

> Parthians, and Medes, and Elamites, and the dwellers in Mesopotamia, and in Judaea, and Cappadocia, in Pontus, and Asia, Phrygia, and Pamphylia, in Egypt, and in the parts of Libya about Cyrene, and strangers of Rome, Jews and proselytes, Cretes and Arabians (vv.9-11).

But they remind us, too, of the immense value of the written Word of God, of the 'scriptures of the prophets'.

The immensity, intricacy, and irresistibility of God's grand purpose will cause us to worship if we grasp but a part of it. But when we think of the darkness in which we would have groped had He never spoken, when we think of the wonder of the Scripture by which He has made His purpose known, when we think of the unique perspective given to us in this dispensation of grace, surely our worship must swell further and rise higher to the unknowable God Who in grace has made Himself known. Let us never take our Bibles for granted, but let us constantly thank God that 'that which is perfect has come' (1 Cor. 13), that we can hold in our hands the complete Word of God, in all of its sufficiency. And let us never cease to worship the God Who has revealed Himself, and made manifest His glorious plan of redemption.

In Galatians 1:3–5 we find another doxology that centres on Divine purpose. But here the focus is not so much on the great historical sweep of God's plan as with the central and singular event that it involved:

> Grace be to you and peace from God the Father, and from our Lord Jesus Christ, Who gave Himself for our sins, that He might deliver us from this present evil world, according to the will of God and our Father: To Whom be glory for ever and ever. Amen.

God's redemptive programme is embraced in this short portion. But here the apostle is not specifically occupied, as he was in Romans, with the long overview of the outworkings of God's design. Rather his focus is on the immensity of the central person and the central event of that eternal plan – 'our Lord Jesus Christ' 'gave Himself for us'. So simply expressed, and yet so profoundly significant, this event is the focal point and the fulcrum of history. Lord's Day by Lord's Day, we occupy our minds with this event, as in obedience to the Lord's command we 'shew the Lord's death until He come' (1 Cor. 11:26), and remember that 'He gave Himself for us'. Throughout the week, this tremendous truth ought never to be far from our minds – 'He gave Himself for us'. And though we remember and commemorate it every week, and though it occupies our minds from day-to-day we need never fear that we will deplete its significance. Eternity itself neither will nor can exhaust the tremendous worth of the fact that 'He gave Himself', or the wonder that 'He gave Himself for us'.

The Doxologies and Divine Persons

Worship will be produced by meditating upon the grandeur of Divine purpose and the greatness of Divine power. The third great catalyst of worship in the epistles is the consideration of Divine persons. In these doxologies we have tremendous expressions of theological teaching, packing a profound immensity of truth into a very few words. But these are no dryly academic theological disquisitions. Rather, these vital truths about the greatness of God reach the hearts and souls of the apostles, resulting in true worship. To borrow Lilley's comments on 1 Timothy 1:17, in these portions of Scripture 'the heart of [the] theologian beats with the pulse of a psalmist'.[*]

In Romans 1, God is worshipped as Creator. Paul outlines the tragic record of man's rejection of God's revelation and their repudiation of His person. Although Creation manifest 'His eternal power and Godhead', mankind rejected its testimony, and settled

---

[*] J.P. Lilley, *The Pastoral Epistles*, (Edinburgh: T. &. T. Clark, 1901), 83.

for a distorted understanding of God, and a depraved life. That rejection brought judgement. First their bodies, then their affections, and finally their intellects were given over to evil. It is a tragic tale, the sorrowful and shadowy story of humanity's descent into darkness. But amidst the gloom there shines a bright ray of worship. Even as he recounts the record of abject failure and abounding wickedness, Paul cannot speak of the greatness of Creation without turning his heart to heaven and worshiping 'the Creator, Who is blessed for ever. Amen' (Rom. 1:25).

Man still fails to acknowledge and worship the Creator. Idolatrous religion may have given way to intellectual materialism, and the adoration of false gods have been replaced with the acclaim of false theories. The ultimate result, however, is little different. Still, God is robbed of the worship that rightfully belongs to the Creator Who is revealed in the vastness and intricacy, the elegance and complexity of Creation. The psalmist wondered at 'the heavens, the work of [His] fingers' (Ps. 8:3). Since then, scientific discovery has opened vast and varied vistas that call for our wondering worship. In spite of the practice of our society, and in spite of the pressure that it brings to bear upon us, let us never fail to worship 'the Creator, Who is blessed for ever.'

My soul, thy great Creator praise:
When clothed in His celestial rays,
He in full majesty appears,
And, like a robe, His glory wears.

The heav'ns for His curtains spread,
The unfathomed deep He makes His bed.
Clouds are His chariot when He flies
On wingèd storms across the skies.

> *The world's foundations by His hand*
> *Are poised, and shall for ever stand;*
> *He binds the ocean in His chain,*
> *Lest it should drown the earth again.*
>
> *How strange Thy works! How great Thy skill!*
> *And every land Thy riches fill:*
> *Thy wisdom round the world we see,*
> *This spacious earth is full of Thee.*
> *   –Isaac Watts*

Later in the same epistle, we find another example of worship flashing forth against a most gloomy background. In the opening verses of Romans 9 Paul speaks of his 'great heaviness and continual sorrow' because of the unbelief of Israel. The dark verses are devoid of either happiness or joy. And yet, even in the midst of his sorrow, the Apostle is moved to worship, and to give expression to a vital statement of both the humanity and the Deity of the Lord Jesus Christ:

> Whose are the fathers, and of whom as concerning the flesh Christ came, Who is over all, God blessed for ever. Amen (Rom. 9:5).

Paul's worship here is not the mere overflow of positive feelings, or even the expression of thankfulness for blessings received. Israel has been set aside, Paul could wish himself accursed, but even the deep sorrow that Paul feels and of which he so movingly speaks cannot staunch his worship of the One Who became man, but 'Who is over all, the eternally blessed God' (NKJV). Weeping and worship were not incompatible in the experience of the Apostle Paul, nor should they be in ours. God's greatness does not fluctuate with our feelings, and He remains at all times worthy of our worship.

The first epistle to Timothy is bookended by two great theological doxologies. The first, in chapter one, is connected with the first advent of the Lord Jesus Christ, the other, in chapter six, with His second coming. Both of these doxologies emphasise the eternity, authority, and incorruptibility of God, in contrast to the corrupting influence of false teachers, 'deceiving spirits and teachings of demons' (1 Tim. 4:1 *Darby*).

The first of these doxologies is the briefer of the two. It follows verses where Paul expresses his amazement and thanksgiving that the abundant grace of God had not only been demonstrated by the fact that 'Christ Jesus came into the World to save sinners' (1 Tim. 1:15), but that he, himself, though 'a blasphemer, and a persecutor, and injurious' (v.13) has not only been saved, but has been put 'into the ministry' (v.12). As the apostle traces what God has done, thanksgiving produces worship, and Paul produces a doxology expressing the greatness of God:

> Now unto the King eternal, immortal, invisible, the only wise God, be honour and glory for ever and ever. Amen (1 Tim. 1:17).

Commentators have differed over whether this doxology applies only to God the Father, or only to God the Son, or to the Godhead generally. In view of the content of this doxology and its links with other portions of Scripture, the latter view seems most persuasive: 'the One worshipped is God: there is no need to distinguish persons.'[*]

---

[*] J. Allen, *What the Bible Teaches: I Timothy*, (Kilmarnock: John Ritchie, 1983), 189

The word king used here is the normal term applied to earthly monarchs, and some commentators have seen the phrase as a criticism of emperor worship, and it is implicitly that. But Paul is not interested in comparisons here. Rather, he is stressing the uniqueness of this eternal King, Who stands in contrast to every human monarch. This title 'King' is modified by the three following words, all of which, alliterative aficionados will be pleased to note, begin with the Greek letter *a*, and by the concluding phrase 'the only wise God.' This verse is the only place in the Authorised Version where the expression 'the King eternal' ('the King of the Ages', JND) is used – some manuscripts also have the phrase at Revelation 15:3. Translated as 'the King eternal', this expression reminds us that God is outside of time. Translated as 'the King of the Ages', it reminds us that God is in control of time. One reading implies the other. The fact that God is outside of time, unaffected by its passage, or the vicissitudes that it brings, means that He alone is qualified to control time. His sovereignty is seen in the unfolding of the ages, in the rise and fall of empires, in the variegated unfolding of history. As the 'eternal King' He is neither constrained by time nor limited by weakness, He is boundless in His eternal might.

As our English translation reflects, the following two expressions – 'immortal' (or 'incorruptible') and 'invisible' – both begin with negative prefixes. They tell us what God is not – not corruptible and not visible. These negatives convey not just specific attributes of God, but also His absolute uniqueness, His distinction from all others. None can compare to Him, and Paul's use of these 'negative predicates' marks off His separation from all weakness or limitation.

Thus, Paul goes beyond his statement of God's eternity to affirm His immortality. God is free from any trace of corruption, from either the seeds or the fruit of decline. The expression used in 1 Timothy is only elsewhere used of God in Romans 1:23. The God Who did not begin, and will not end, does not change. What He has been, He is, and always will be. His words to Israel are still true: 'I am the LORD, I change not' (Mal. 3:6).

Thirdly, Paul mentions God's invisibility. God had warned Moses 'Thou canst not see my face: for there shall no man see me, and live' (Exod. 33:20), and restricted him to a view of the afterglow of Divine glory. Even the reflected glory of God in the face of Moses was so great 'that the children of Israel could not stedfastly behold the face of Moses for the glory of his countenance' (2 Cor. 3:7). In John 5, the Lord Jesus reminded Jews that they had not 'seen [God's] shape' (5:37), and, in the following chapter, He again stressed that no-one 'hath seen the Father, save He which is of God' (6:46). Colossians 1:15 tells us that He is 'the invisible God'. In contrast to the tangible idols venerated by a pagan world, God transcends our senses. It is precious to note that almost every New Testament reference to the invisibility of God is followed by a statement of His revelation in Christ, and we rejoice in the One Who is the 'image of the invisible God' (Col. 1:15), 'the brightness of His glory, and the express image of His person' (Heb. 1:3). The only exception to this rule is this passage, and a moment's consideration will reveal that it is only an apparent exception. This doxology follows Paul's statement that 'Christ Jesus came into the world', his statement that he is the object lesson in whom 'Jesus Christ' is showing 'all longsuffering'. The invisibility of God does not mean that we need to resort to any gnostic imaginings, philosophical speculations, or theological despair for 'God, who commanded the light to shine out of darkness, hath shined in our hearts, to give the light of the knowledge of the glory of God in the face of Jesus Christ' (2 Cor. 4:6).

Paul draws his catalogue of Divine attributes to a close with the phrase rendered in the Authorised as 'the only wise God'. There is good manuscript support for the translation 'only God' (*Darby*) and, while both are true, the latter rendering seems to fit most neatly with the context. Paul is not just extolling the uniqueness of God's wisdom, he is affirming the uniqueness of God. Amidst the polytheism of his day, and the inroads being made amongst Christians by gnostic error that postulated degrees of deity, Paul states clearly and unequivocally the truth attested in all of Scripture: 'the LORD our God is one LORD' (Deut. 6:4).

And so Paul closes his doxology. And he moves immediately to Timothy's responsibility:

> This charge I commit unto thee, son Timothy, according to the prophecies which went before on thee, that thou by them mightest war a good warfare' (v.18).

Worship will lead to work and to warfare. Paul's charge to Timothy would have been a sober one in any context. But here, with the Apostle's words of worship ringing in our ears, it acquires an even greater weight. Once again, we see that worship is the tie that binds together theology and practice. Doctrine cannot pass from our head to our feet without going through our heart.

Before he finishes his letter, the Apostle breaks once more into worship. Chapter 6:15–16 contain another doxology:

> Who is the blessed and only Potentate, the King of kings, and Lord of lords; Who only hath immortality, dwelling in the light which no man can approach unto; Whom no man hath seen, nor can see: to Whom be honour and power everlasting. Amen (1 Tim. 6:15–16).

This doxology is so closely linked with chapter 1:17. It is fair to say that this doxology is an expansion of the earlier prayer. As outlined below, the parallels of thought between the two passages are striking:

1 Tim. 1:17	1 Tim. 6:15–16
'the King eternal'	'the blessed and only Potentate, the King of kings, and Lord of lords'
Immortal	'Who only hath immortality'
Invisible	'dwelling in light which no man can approach unto; Whom no man hath seen, nor can see'

Notice, however, that the second doxology does not simply repeat the first. Rather, each element of the first is expanded upon in the second. So 'the king eternal' is expanded into the glorious title 'the blessed and only Potentate, the King of kings, and the Lord of lords. Here again, God's sovereignty is stressed. In these verses, Paul emphasises God's control over the course of history. The manifestation of the Lord Jesus Christ will take place 'in His own time', fully in accordance with the Divine timetable. In chapter 1, it was the duration of God's sovereignty that was noted – 'the king eternal'. Here it is the extent of that sovereignty – He is the only Potentate, the King over kings, and the Lord over lords

Similarly, the truth of Divine immortality is reiterated. Here the word used is different to the 'incorruptible' of chapter one. Here Paul states the truth that God is deathless, that He is not and cannot be subject to death. This is identified as a unique and essential quality of Deity. He imparts eternal life to His own, and the day is coming what 'this mortal [will] put on immortality' (1 Cor. 15:53), but as an essential quality it belongs to God alone.

The invisibility of God, too, is expanded upon in these verses. We have already seen that this attribute marks God out as transcendent, beyond the scope of our senses. Here we learn that it is His glory that renders Him invisible. He dwells 'in light unapproachable', in the blinding radiance of His manifest excellence. The impact of a glimpse of this glory in the risen Lord Jesus was 'a light ... above the brightness of the sun', which brought Saul of Tarsus to the ground. It was such that John 'fell at His feet as dead' (Rev. 1:17). Just as our eyes do not have the capacity to look upon the sun without permanent damage, human flesh cannot tolerate the intensity and brilliance of the 'light unapproachable' in which God dwells.

These are tremendous truths. But there is a simple, but very profound, lesson that we can learn from the way in which this second doxology develops the first. The development of worship in these verses reminds us that we will never exhaust the greatness of God. At the beginning of the epistle, Paul's heart was moved to worship by the contemplation of three of the innumerable attributes of God. Now, at the end of the epistle, it is the very same attributes that provoke him to praise. But he is not merely restating what he had earlier expressed. Now he is expressing a deeper appreciation of each of these Divine features. We can learn from his example. We would never want our worship to be maggoty manna, the stale repetition of the same thoughts over and over again. But this does not mean that we cannot meditate again and again on the glories of our God, gaining a deeper understanding of His unique greatness, and finding our worship becoming ever deeper and more detailed.

We should also note that this doxology, too, is followed by a series of solemn charges for Timothy and for those among whom he served. Once again we are reminded of the practical and ethical implications of worship, of its power to motivate committed Christian living.

It is interesting to notice the contrast between these doxologies, and the account of humanity's failure given in Romans 1. In that great indictment of mankind, it is precisely the characteristics of God outlined in these verses that were rejected by mankind. They refused to worship the God Whose invisible glories were manifest in creation:

> For the invisible things ['His invisible attributes' ESV] of Him from the creation of the world are clearly seen, being understood by the things that are made, even His eternal power and Godhead; so that they are without excuse: Because that, when they knew God, they glorified Him not as God, neither were thankful but became vain in their imaginations, and their foolish heart was darkened. Professing themselves to be wise, they became fools, And changed the glory of the uncorruptible God into an image made like to

corruptible man, and to birds, and fourfooted beasts, and creeping things (Rom. 1:20–23).

So the Divine attributes that Paul mentions 1 Timothy, those attributes that prompt his doxologies are precisely those that fallen man fails to recognise. God is too great for their minds, too transcendent for their sinful consciousness. So rather than give Him what is His due, they imagine tangible, temporal gods, and worship them, rather than 'the only God'.

Notice the terms in which Paul speaks of their failure: 'they glorified Him not as God'. The word 'glorified' has as its root word *doxa*, the same word of glory that is found in each of the doxologies. The world at large has no doxology for God. But by His grace, we have been brought to acknowledge what fallen humanity rejected and denied. Meditating upon the greatness of God moves us not to fear and denial, but to reverence and to worship – to glorify Him as God, and to be thankful. But we are not immune to the temptation to scale God down, to lose our appreciation of the greatness and uniqueness of His person. May God grant that we will have right thoughts of Himself, and that the song of our souls will in truth be 'how great Thou art'.

These doxologies will abundantly repay our careful consideration. To unpack their concentrated teaching about the manifold greatness of Divine power, Divine purpose, and Divine persons is a vast but immensely valuable task. As we consider these exemplars of worship, may our hearts be moved to join with the Apostles', and to ascribe glory to Him, for ever and ever.

This chapter does not, by any means, offer exhaustive survey of New Testament doxologies. In particular, by focusing on the epistles, we have excluded the great doxologies recorded in the book of Revelation. These, too, will reward the careful student.

Before bringing this chapter, and this book to a close, however, there is one other doxology that should be mentioned. Drawing his second epistle to its conclusion, the Apostle Peter penned words of encouragement, exhortation, and of worship:

> But grow in grace, and in the knowledge of our Lord and Saviour Jesus Christ. To Him be glory both now and for ever ['and to the day of eternity' *Darby*]. Amen (2 Pet. 3:18).

With these beautiful words the Apostle expresses the desire of his heart for his readers. That desire is simply stated, and yet he could have envisaged no higher aspiration. And having expressed his desire for the believer, his last inspired words are an expression of worship, of the desire that glory be ascribed to our Lord and Saviour Jesus Christ now, and to the day of eternity. His closing phrase, unique in Scripture, opens before us a glorious vista, of an unending, never-dwindling, eternal day, in which 'He shall bear the glory' (Zech. 6:13). What a day, what a glorious day, that will be. And, in the 'now', until it dawns, let us 'give unto the LORD the glory due unto His name; worship the LORD in the beauty of holiness' (Ps. 29:2).